Developing Effective Classroom Groups

A PRACTICAL GUIDE FOR TEACHERS

GENE STANFORD

A HART BOOK

A & W VISUAL LIBRARY • NEW YORK

For Barbara, with love

Published in 1980 by
A&W Publishers, Inc.
95 Madison Avenue
New York, New York 10016

Library of Congress Catalog Card Number: 80-65595

ISBN: 0-89104-188-5

Printed in Canada

PREFACE

A classroom full of people is not necessarily a group. The individuals may have no sense of group identity. If they are not comfortable with one another, they hesitate to contribute much for fear of ridicule or embarrassment. Usually they compete with one another fiercely. When they can be induced to cooperate, their efforts are frequently ineffective because they lack the skills necessary for working together cooperatively.

To become a group this classroom of individuals must undergo certain changes. It must, in effect, mature. Sometimes a class develops into a group with a minimum of intervention from the teacher. Sometimes this evolution takes place smoothly and effortlessly; almost magically a class becomes an effective working unit.

But most classes never develop into groups. Nothing happens to push them toward maturity. They remain a collection of individuals, lacking the attitudes and skills needed to work together effectively. As a result, class discussions rarely get off the ground, and group projects fail disastrously. Students resist group tasks. No one feels very good about spending time together each day.

Most teachers have some vague notions about the principles of group dynamics. They know something about the need for cohesiveness, about the importance of having all members of a group contribute, about democratic versus authoritarian leadership. They sense that their collection of individuals must develop a group identity.

But usually they know very little about how a teacher can deliberately intervene to help a group develop. Most books on group dynamics explain clearly what *ought* to happen in a group, but rarely do they suggest in practical terms how a teacher can bring about that ideal state.

In this book I have tried to provide practical, how-to-do-it material on group dynamics that a teacher can use in a classroom. I have not ignored the theoretical principles necessary for understanding why such activities are useful, but my primary goal is to suggest the means through which a teacher can bring about the desired changes, rather than just admonishing the teacher to do so. In a sense, I've tried to create a technology for implementing the science of group behavior.

At the heart of this technology are *structured experiences*. These are carefully devised learning activities that the teacher uses to introduce students to a new skill or attitude, or to alter the classroom climate in some way. I do not believe that a group can develop simply by having the teacher model the desired behavior. The behavior of the group members must change, and this can be done most expeditiously through the use of carefully planned, structured learning activities and experiences.

My approach to group development is derived to a great extent from my experience as an English teacher at Horton Watkins High School in Ladue, Missouri. Initially I thought that the personality of the teacher was solely responsible for the quality of student interaction in the classroom. I believed that if a teacher was open, honest, sensitive, understanding, and willing to give students the freedom to be themselves, good group process was sure to result. To a certain extent I was right. By displaying these characteristics, I encouraged students to open up somewhat and interact more freely.

But many difficulties remained unresolved. For example, although students were generally happy to interact freely with me, they continued to be defensive with one another. They had trouble discussing a topic when I did not serve as leader of the group, and they did not listen closely when other people talked in class.

Thus I came to believe that more than just the personal characteristics of the teacher was involved in improving the functioning of the classroom group. Not only do students need to observe the desired behavior, but they also need to practice it. I started introducing into my class structured activities to change the behavior of the students. During one school year, I tested the effects of these activities by systematically using them with some groups and not with others. The outcome of the experiment convinced me that training activities can be a key factor in successfully merging a class into an effective group.

During my experiment I had asked my students to keep a journal in which they were to record their impressions of what was happening to them personally and to their class. Most students kept only sketchy records. But one student, Janet Madden, turned in a candid, detailed log of her reactions to the experiences in group development. With her permission, I have quoted from it liberally throughout this book as I think it gives a vivid account of a student's perception of group development in the classroom.

Encouraged by my results, I continued to develop additional training activities and to implement them with classroom groups. But I was nagged by doubt. How could I be sure that the groups were developing because of the training activities and not because of my own personal characteristics? Could any teacher be successful with this approach—or only those with particular personal qualities?

To answer these questions, I put together a set of the thirty most essential training exercises and recruited nineteen junior high school teachers of various subjects who were willing to use these exercises with their classes. The success reported by these teachers suggests that the development of effective groups depends not on any special traits of the teacher, but on the teacher's willingness to utilize certain procedures and activities in the classroom.

The suggestions contained in this book are the result of my own personal experience and the experience of other teachers I have worked with. I used many of these ideas successfully long before I learned the theoretical reasons for *why* they work. I know that the activities can work in a variety of situations, and can be used successfully by teachers who vary greatly in personality. I firmly believe that anyone who is willing can follow these instructions and help his class become more effective as a group.

Of course, the teacher who is more democratic by nature is likely to be more successful than one who is authoritarian. A teacher who likes and accepts young people will be more successful than one who is critical and suspicious. And the teacher who has had some training in group dynamics will probably be more successful, too. But this book was not written for paragons. It was written for the average teacher, who has the usual human limitations and no special virtues, but who wants to improve the functioning of a classroom group.

Although most of what I have to say in these pages is based on my own experience as a teacher, I owe a great deal of my knowledge about group development to other sources. Considerable research has been conducted and reported as to the way groups change over time. Even though few of the groups studied were classroom groups, these research findings have contributed to my own concepts of group development in the classroom. It was from my friend and teacher, Albert E. Roark of the University of Colorado, that I first learned the importance of concepts of group development. He will recognize in almost every section of this book his influence on my thinking.

Barbara Stiltner and I worked jointly on research in group development in the classroom. Her efforts were among the very first to test the empirical application of theories of group development in secondary school classes. Besides sharing in her research findings, I learned much and grew in many ways because of my association with her.

I am also indebted to John Jones and William Pfeiffer of University Associates, who were among the first to systematically organize and disseminate structured experiences for use in human relations training. A number of the activities in this book are adaptations of material from their handbooks and I am grateful to them for having had access to their fine work.

I am deeply grateful to Janet Madden for allowing me to quote extensively from the personal journal she kept while she was a student in my class. She wrote her comments never supposing that they would be made public, and since they do not always portray her or me in the most favorable light, I'm sure it took courage for her to grant me permission to quote them.

Also, I acknowledge the contributions to this project made by Richard and Patricia Schmuck, who carefully reviewed the manuscript and made suggestions for improvement. Although they are in no way to be held responsible for the content of this book, their help was invaluable.

Most important, it was from my wife Barbara that I first learned about the possibility of using training activities to help students learn the skills needed for effective group work. Had she not included me in the creative work she was doing in teaching discussion skills to her high school students, I probably would never have developed my present interest in group development. Her contribution to this book goes beyond the usual "unending patience, good coffee, and help in typing the manuscript" acknowledged of their wives by most male authors. In fact, come to think of it, she makes atrocious coffee and has never once offered to type a manuscript.

GENE STANFORD

Utica, New York
January 1, 1977

CONTENTS

CHAPTER 4.   STAGE TWO: ESTABLISHING
NORMS—*Goal 2: Responding to Others*

CHAPTER 10. STAGE FIVE: TERMINATION

Developing Effective
Classroom Groups

1 THE CLASSROOM AS A GROUP

"I hear you're teaching with group dynamics," Marianne Lasky said to me cheerfully. "Sometime I'd like to borrow your lesson plans and try it out. I'm always looking for a way to vary the routine."

Before I could respond, Bill Haywood—a fellow English teacher—interrupted. "I hear he's been having kids talk about their personal lives," he told Marianne. "I'm just waiting to hear a report that they've started taking off their clothes like in one of those encounter groups," he said with a smirk and a wink.

We were sitting in the faculty lounge during the period designated "planning," in which we rarely had time to do more than drink a cup of coffee, check the mailbox, and fortify ourselves for the rest of the day.

I was used to Bill's cracks about my classes. He knew very well what I was doing and why, but he insisted on portraying me as some sort of panderer or worse. His joking— while occasionally annoying—I could live with. But there was something about Marianne's view of group dynamics that I found troublesome.

Patiently, I started to explain that group dynamics is not some sort of gimmick that can be used to provide a change of pace when the kids get fed up with reading or listening to the teacher. I tried to point out that group dynamics is not a teaching method on a par with lecture, role-play, discussion, or recitation, but a set of principles to consider no matter what method the teacher is using.

I must have really gotten carried away, because at least four other teachers wandered over, overhearing my "speech" to Marianne and wondering what was going on.

"Is this group dynamics stuff the same as small group instruction?" Clarence Matthews asked. "At Parkway, where I taught last year, we had a big push for small groups. The principal said we ought to stop lecturing so much."

"Well," I began, "the use of small groups in the classroom certainly draws on the theories of group dynamics . . ."

"Why don't you just admit," Bill interrupted again, "that your primary purpose is to get the kids to talk about their sex lives?"

He may have been kidding, but it made me bristle. And it didn't help any when Edna Watson (who never let me forget that her 15 years' teaching experience made her more competent than I was, with only two) added, "Yes, what is this sensitivity training you've been doing, anyway?"

I forced a smile and answered, as calmly as I could, "I'm not doing sensitivity training; I'm not having kids talk about their sex lives; and I'm not experimenting with some new-fangled teaching method. I'm just trying to put into practice some basic principles of group process to give my classroom a more pleasant atmosphere and make learning more effective."

Bill couldn't resist another attempt at humor: "May I suggest that a good first step toward improving your class-room atmosphere would be to convince Jed Ostrow that he ought to use deodorant occasionally?"

The others laughed heartily, and before I could complete my reply to Marianne, the bell was ringing and we all had to rush to third-hour classes.

GROUP DYNAMICS

The questions raised by my colleagues at that school are the same questions that I hear now from other teachers I meet at conferences and professional meetings. Group dynamics, many assume, is a new teaching method that gives students a chance to talk to one another a lot, and encourages students to undertake group projects on topics that they, not the teacher, have chosen. Some teachers think that group dynamics is somehow the same as "touch-and-tell," T-groups, and sensitivity training. Others think group dynamics implies constant small group discussions, or student-centered learning, or an end to individualized instruction. But it isn't any of these things.

Group dynamics examines the way people behave in groups and attempts to understand the factors that make a group more effective. It looks at different styles of leadership and patterns of influence, at the processes by which decisions are made in the group, at the norms—that is, ideas of what is appropriate behavior or appropriate procedures—in the group, at the pattern of communication in the group, and at factors such as openness and cohesiveness. Since the early 1950s, scores of research studies have provided us with new information identifying the characteristics that make groups more effective and provide their members with maximum satisfaction. This information can be utilized by the teacher to promote learning, to prevent "discipline" problems, and to promote the personal growth of the individual student.[1]

---

[1]Since this book is intended to be practical, theoretical material has been kept to a minimum. The reader who wishes more theoretical background information on group dynamics is referred to *Group Processes in the Classroom* by Richard A. Schmuck and Patricia A. Schmuck, Dubuque, Iowa: Wm. C. Brown Company, 1971.

BECOMING AN EFFECTIVE GROUP

Effective classroom groups share certain characteristics:

(1) The members understand and accept one another.

(2) Communication is open.

(3) Members take responsibility for their own learning and behavior.

(4) Members cooperate.

(5) Processes for making decisions have been established.

(6) Members are able to confront problems openly and resolve their conflicts constructively.

Effective classroom groups, in short, are productive working units.

Groups like this don't just happen; they have to be carefully nurtured. To create an effective group, the teacher must understand the problems that groups commonly face throughout their time together. The teacher needs skill and patience to lead the group through the maze of developmental problems it will face.

The process whereby a collection of individuals (sometimes referred to as an *aggregate*) changes into a *group* is known as group development. Changing a collection of individual students into an effective class group comes about only by teacher intervention to promote group development. In this process, the individuals learn more productive ways of working together, develop trust in one another, become open to new experiences, improve their communication, and feel freer to participate actively in classroom activities.

Developing from an aggregate into a group closely parallels the process of developing from an infant into a mature adult. As writers such as Erikson[2] and Havighurst[3] have emphasized, the human being goes through successive stages of development. At each stage the person must learn to cope with new problems and must develop new skills and attitudes. After mastering each of these stages, the individual may arrive at mature adulthood.

Similarly, a collection of individuals in a classroom must undergo successive changes in order to reach the stage of a productive working unit. The class must confront problems openly as they occur, and develop new skills and attitudes in response to them. Many human beings fail to grow up socially and emotionally, and many classes fail to develop into effective working units.

THE STAGES OF GROUP DEVELOPMENT

The following is a brief outline of the five stages (see chart on page 31) through which a group would ideally move when the teacher intervenes to maximize their group development.[4] Each of these stages is described in detail in subsequent chapters of this book.

Stage One: Orientation.

When students enter the classroom on the first day they are full of questions, most of which indicate a need to understand what this new situation is going to be like ("Will we have to write book reports?" "How many A's do you give?"

---

[2]Erikson, E. H. *Childhood and Society.* New York: W. W. Norton and Co., 1964.

[3]Havighurst, R. J. *Developmental Tasks and Education* (3rd ed.). New York: David McKay, 1972.

[4]For the rationale for this conceptualization of the stages of group development, see the Appendix, page 280.

"Do we have to keep a notebook?") and who the other people are. Students are concerned about how they are going to be treated by both the teacher and the other students, and how they are going to fit into the classroom group. Group development interventions during the early days focus on describing what students can expect to happen in the class, and on getting members of the class acquainted with one another.

Stage Two: Establishing Norms.

After a few days, or a few weeks, of orientation activities, students begin to work out norms for future behavior. These norms are the shared expectations of how members should act in the group. The teacher can intervene to assure that the norms that are established are those that are likely to be most helpful to the group.

1.   **Group Responsibility.**   The first of these norms is that the group takes responsibility for its own functioning. Individual members agree to take responsibility to contribute to group activity. Members take responsibility for calling on others to contribute. Members take varying degrees of responsibility for leadership of the group. The group begins to work together independent of direct supervision by the teacher.

2.   **Responsiveness to Others.**   A second norm that must be established early is that students listen carefully to each other and respond to one another. In most classes, when there is a discussion the exchange is between the teacher and the students. The students may react to the teacher's comments, but it is expected that the teacher will do most of the responding to the students. When students react to one another, it is often regarded as disruptive. So students have come to tune out to each other and to treat each other's contributions with a lack of respect or serious consideration. It is important to free and train students to interact directly with

THE TIME SEQUENCE

It may have appeared from the description in this outline that the stages of group development are discrete and mutually exclusive. In reality they overlap to a great extent. For example, the teacher may decide to continue orientation activities for several weeks, but at the same time start the process of establishing norms. Similarly, a group just entering the Productivity Stage may continue to face occasional conflict. In short, it is very difficult to pinpoint exactly how long it should take to complete a stage, or when a class should move from one stage to the next.

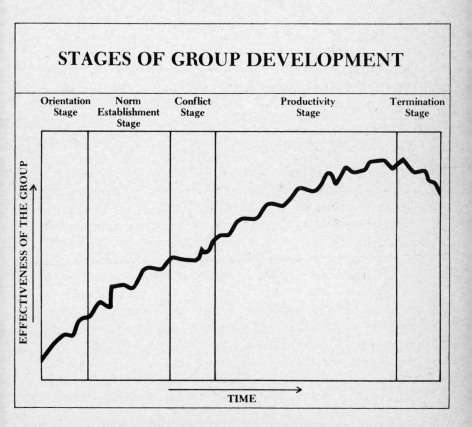

STAGES OF GROUP DEVELOPMENT

| Orientation Stage | Norm Establishment Stage | Conflict Stage | Productivity Stage | Termination Stage |

EFFECTIVENESS OF THE GROUP

TIME

It is important to note that the amount of time a specific group will require for each stage cannot be prescribed. Some classes reach maturity more quickly than others. Also, the amount of time a class will spend at each stage will be different depending on how long the class stays together. A class that meets for a full year might expect to spend two weeks in the Termination Stage, whereas students in a three-week mini-course may go through termination in a single day.

The chart, Stages of Group Development, indicates the sequence of stages and degree of group effectiveness at successive stages. The time spans are relative and show the usual proportion of time for one stage compared to another. As a general rule of thumb, the teacher should expect to be moving the class through the first three stages during the first six to eight weeks, assuming that the class meets for approximately an hour daily. I've rarely seen a group take less time to reach productivity, but it is quite usual for it to take longer. Although it is desirable, of course, to spend the bulk of the school year in the Productivity Stage, each stage provides necessary and satisfying learning experiences.

It should not be inferred from the chart or outline that the process of group development is neat and orderly. Group development requires the teacher to introduce certain interventions in roughly sequential order—that is, certain things need to happen early in the life of the class, other things shouldn't be expected until later; some skills need to be taught before others, because some skills build on those developed earlier. But this does not mean that once the class has completed a developmental stage it will never again need to deal with issues that characterize that stage. In fact, good groups never really finish dealing with earlier issues; they come back to them periodically, although each time they are able to deal with them in a more sophisticated fashion.

For example, an important issue of the Orientation Stage is "Who are the people here?" Weeks, even months, after the class has left this stage behind, the students will come back to this issue and will get to know one another in ever greater depth. The issue of "What is my place in this group?" occurs initially in the Orientation Stage, but crops up again in the Norm Establishment Stage when the group develops patterns of leadership and influence.

Thus, the process of group development is *cyclical* as well as sequential. Virtually every problem or concern that the group faces, or skill that its members develop, plays a part in some later stage of development. As though they were climbing a spiral staircase, the students come back to the same issues, but each time at a higher level. The suggestions in this book are arranged according to a rough time sequence, but this is not a "schedule" to be maintained at all costs. You should not feel discouraged if you find you need to return to suggestions from a previous stage because the group is still confronting earlier issues.

ADVANTAGES OF DEVELOPING EFFECTIVE GROUPS

Is the process of group development really worth the time and effort? Why should a teacher bother getting students acquainted with one another? Don't they do that themselves between classes or at lunch or on the playground? Why not just let things take their natural course?

It's a temptation to claim that group development can revolutionize education, but all of us know that no single educational practice can make us 100 per cent successful. Nevertheless, it is possible to speak very confidently about the potential benefits that group development can provide. Intervening to facilitate the transformation of a classroom of individuals into a productive group can make a significant difference in the lives of students in the class. It can yield benefits ranging from better grades on tests to better interpersonal relationships.

Improved Subject-Matter Learning.

Without a doubt, the class that has been helped to develop into a mature group learns more. This is so for a variety of reasons.

First, group development reduces the level of threat in the classroom, making students more comfortable with one another and less defensive. Threat—whether it be fear of embarrassment or ridicule, fear of a low grade, or concern about gaining the teacher's approval—causes students to defend themselves psychologically, and the most common defense is to close themselves off. Students who are defending themselves against threat are not open to learning. It's only when they feel comfortable enough to let down their protective shields that they can interact freely and constructively with new stimuli.

Second, group development promotes subject-matter learning by freeing students to participate more actively in learning activities. We all know that learning increases when students are actively involved in the learning process. When students are comfortable enough to be responsive, teachers are encouraged to make less use of lecture and other passive methods and to make greater use of discussion, role-playing, and small group projects. Research which I conducted in junior high school classes[5] indicates that participation in class discussions is significantly higher in classes that have been through the process of group development than in comparable classes that have not.

Even though we may be convinced that teaching methods which actively involve the students have advantages, many of us are reluctant to undertake them because we've had unpleasant experiences with them—discussions that never got off the ground, role-playing that flopped, group projects that

---

[5]Stanford, G. "The Effect of Interaction Exercises on the Quality of Class Discussions in Junior High Schools." Unpublished doctoral dissertation, University of Colorado, 1973.

fizzled because students wouldn't take responsibility. I believe that often we fail with these methods because most of them require a fairly well developed classroom group. Role-playing with students who are an aggregate and not a group is almost doomed to failure. When students feel at ease with each other, when they respond to the contributions of others, when they communicate openly and accurately, when they take responsibility for directing themselves, then role-playing and the other active-involvement methods will be successful. Group development is in effect a prerequisite to the implementation of teaching methods that attempt to increase learning through active student involvement.

Finally, group development promotes learning by increasing student-to-student interaction. We are all aware of the strength of peer influence, yet rarely do we utilize this influence to enhance learning. Students are more likely to be open to what they hear from fellow students than to what the teacher tells them. For example, if Tim's arguments contain logical fallacies, it's more likely that he will see the fallacies if they're pointed out by a fellow student than if the teacher attempts to correct him. However, this requires a fairly mature level of group development. Without a program of systematic group development interventions, student-to-student interaction is limited at best and may be disruptive or harmful at worst.

My belief that group development interventions can improve subject-matter learning was confirmed by an experiment I conducted with my own classes. One semester, a standard test was administered to all students in grades 10-12 in my school, and those making below a certain score were required to take a special nine-week course in traditional grammar and usage. I divided my grammar class at random into two groups. One group I taught in the conventional way; with the other group I used a series of group development activities. At the end of the term, all the grammar students took another standard test. All my students improved their scores significantly, but the half of the class that had undergone group development activities during their nine weeks together scored significantly higher than the half taught conventionally.[6]

Improved Classroom Management.

Inattentiveness and misbehavior are problems that plague almost all teachers. We are forced to resort to disciplinary measures of some sort when the learning atmosphere of the classroom has been disrupted. Most of us try to handle misbehavior by focusing on the individual student: we frown, we scold, we punish, we counsel, we cajole. But focusing on the individual troublemakers overlooks the fact that the classroom is a social system, and that each student's behavior influences and is influenced by the others in the class. From the perspective of group development, "discipline" may often be seen as a symptom that something has gone wrong in the group—a topic or lesson is too threatening; a struggle is going on for leadership and status; a student who is continually rejected by the rest of the class is reacting; a breakdown has occurred in communicating clearly. Lectures and punishment do little to alleviate such underlying factors. On the other hand, the activities that promote group development build the skills for coping directly with such problems.

Teachers who have implemented group development approaches usually find that the incidence of misbehavior drops dramatically. Quoted below are comments made by junior high school teachers who participated in a research project (see footnote 5, page 34) to test the effectiveness of group development in the classroom. Each teacher had an experimental class that incorporated group development

---

[6]Stanford, G. "Psychological Education in the Classroom." *Personnel and Guidance Journal*, 50(1972), 585-592.

approaches and a control class that was taught in the conventional way. Here are some of the differences they noted:

> My experimental group is more spontaneous, informal, inter-relating, *self-disciplined*, and able to handle discussion (emphasis added).

> The atmosphere in both classes is good, but in the experimental group there is more unity and less division among students. The experimental group has better discussion skills.

> Experimental: as far as I can determine, for seventh graders their discussion skills are excellent. Rapport is very good, too. Control: poor discussion skills—they don't cooperate to achieve a goal. Atmosphere is generally good, but during a discussion sometimes hostile.

> Experimental group is better able to work as a team toward a goal, is more goal- or task-oriented, needs less teacher direction. My control class is a good group, but they don't have a group unity feeling that my experimental group has. I'm very much impressed with the team spirit my experimental class developed as a result of the [group development] activities. The change in their ability to contribute effectively and their increased sensitivity to each other as persons, their ability to work towards a goal without teacher direction—all made the time spent worthwhile.

> All students in my experimental class have shown at least some working knowledge of discussion skills. Students in control class and I have less easy relationships—even tense at times. In my experimental class, we are freer with one another. Experimental class students are more accepting, tolerant of each other's problems, abilities, and personalities. My control class has negative feelings, hostility often expressed openly toward one another. They are fragmented, can't work as a total group.

Improved Social Skills.

Educational goals have recently reflected increasing attention to the affective, as well as the intellectual, needs of students. Group development activities involve examining and improving communication and interpersonal relations. The comments of the teachers quoted above indicate that group development contributed positively to improved social skills.

From the student's point of view, the changes in interpersonal relations brought about in a class that has achieved advanced stages of group development can be fairly dramatic. Janet Madden was a bright but rather shy tenth grader. When the semester began late in January, she found herself with a new group of students, many of whom, she felt, didn't like school, were hostile toward both the teacher and other students, and were generally uncooperative and disruptive. By May 8, the following entry in Janet's personal journal shows the enormous progress she had made in understanding and relating to classmates who had previously made her feel uncomfortable:

> *Today, Mr. Stanford found out that Shari, Bruce, Mark and I have been having our own group discussions out of class. He was very happy and impressed, but I don't know why. We just want to become much better friends and find out more about each other. That's nothing, Tuesday I took Mark H. and Mike P. to this sports place in Clayton to get hockey sticks. It was really fun. All the kids in the class are so nice and fun to be with.*

Six months after the end of class, Janet wrote me a letter that clearly shows her new social skills:

> *Shari is fine and we're closer than ever. Bruce is really great, too! He calls me about once every two weeks just to talk. We are really close. I see Mark and Lee once in a while. But for the rest, I have lost complete*

> *contact with them. It's really sad and I do miss them.*
> *You know, every time I think about last year and the*
> *"experiment," I get the greatest feeling. You helped*
> *me to learn so much about contact with people. I have*
> *experienced so many different and more involved*
> *relationships this year as a result of what I learned last*
> *year. You made me so happy with people in general.*

Over a year after her experience in the class that had become a group, Janet was no less convinced of its value. In a letter to me, she wrote:

> *After last year, the members of the class tried to*
> *follow your philosophies on people. We went out of*
> *our ways to learn about people and start new relation-*
> *ships with them. After the "experiment" we felt so*
> *good about what had happened. We have learned to*
> *enjoy people more.*

At least in this particular case, group development had effects far beyond making a single class an enjoyable experience for the students or enhancing their learning in that one situation. Group development also imparts basic skills and attitudes in interpersonal relations that students can and do apply long afterwards.

HOW DO I BEGIN?

There are two basic means through which you can promote the development of a class into a group, and both approaches are necessary. The first approach is to alter your own behavior. For example, during the Norm Establishment Stage, you can withdraw from leadership of a discussion, allowing students to assume leadership functions. By structuring classroom procedures in a particular way, you establish certain expectations in the group and give students an opportunity to develop the new skills they need.

Also, you can influence students by modeling, through your own behavior, the behavior you want them to display in the group. If, for example, you want students to develop the habit of looking directly at a person who is speaking, be sure you display this behavior yourself when a student is speaking.

The second approach to group development is to conduct specific learning activities designed to bring about changes in students' attitudes and skills. In effect, you must train students directly in the new behavior you want them to cultivate. You might, for example, describe a step-by-step procedure for resolving a conflict and then have them practice it in role-playing situations. Or you could utilize a simulation game that gives students insight into the importance of cooperation in accomplishing group goals.

In this book both approaches are explained in detail— ways of changing classroom procedures and modeling helpful group membership behavior are described, and structured activities to help students learn new attitudes and skills are provided. For each step of the group development process, new teacher behavior and student exercises are presented.

Assuming that you are convinced of the value of group development, how do you go about implementing the suggestions in the book? First, it is a good idea to read the entire book through once to gain an overall understanding of each stage of group development. Keep in mind the chart on page 31 showing the relative amounts of time to be devoted to each stage.

Then look at each chapter in detail. I have devoted one chapter to each stage in the group development process, except for the Norm Establishment Stage, which is so complex and so crucial that it has been broken down into five chapters, one for each norm to be developed.

Each chapter begins with a description of the characteristics and needs of the group at that stage of development. Next is a description of, and suggestions for, forms of teacher behavior that are most useful during this particular stage of the group's development. Finally, a variety of structured experiences are suggested, designed to bring about changes in students' attitudes or behavior. These experiences range from games to training exercises, and comprise the basic component of the group development program. They are presented in enough detail so that you can implement them without any prior training in group dynamics.

Whenever possible, I have attempted to suggest ways in which group development can be fostered using the subject matter of the course as a basis. By adapting the format of structured experiences to the course content, you can achieve group development goals at the same time that you are teaching subject matter. Students, as well as teachers, seem to be more comfortable if they can see the relationship between group activity and the specific goals of the course.

Group development activities are best undertaken as an integral part of the class program, not as a gimmick tacked on as an afterthought. This involves the careful integration of group development activities into daily and unit lesson plans. Giving attention to the effectiveness of the class as a group should become as natural a class goal as is individual mastery of skills in subject matter.

2 STAGE ONE: ORIENTATION

"English 10—Stanford—Room 104," Janet read from her computer-printed schedule slip. "I wonder what we're going to do in English this year. I hope we don't do oral book reports or speeches. I'll just die if I have to get up in front of the class like last year."

Janet headed down the hall toward Room 104. "I wonder what Mr. Stanford's like," she thought. "He's looked nice enough when I've seen him in the hall, but I've heard that the kids spend a lot of time discussing things in his class. I hope some of my friends will be there so I won't be afraid to talk. If he thinks that discussion is important, he might give me a bad grade if I can't get up my nerve to talk. . . . Leslie was in his class last year. She said that she made a lot of friends in the class. That sure would be nice."

By this time Janet had arrived at Room 104. "Oh, no!" she thought, and she quickly changed direction and headed for the water fountain across the hall. "There's Mike P. I hope he doesn't tease me like he did last year in algebra. I'm going to sit on the opposite side of the room from him and maybe he'll find someone else to pick on."

Finally, Janet could avoid the room no longer. Inside, she found the desks arranged in one large circle. And there was no one she knew very well. "Oh, dear, where should I sit?" she thought. "There's an empty seat beside Shari What's-Her-Name from last year's gym class. She's the only person I even kind of know and like. But what if I sit beside her and then one of her real friends comes in? Hey, there's Bruce H. I wish I had the nerve to sit by him. . . . I've got to sit down fast before Mike notices me. I guess I'll sit by Shari."

Shari did not look up as Janet approached and sat down. Janet wanted to say hello, but instead she looked around the room. She felt vaguely uncomfortable in the circle. There was no place to hide—she could see everyone and they could see her. Two boys—who Janet was later to learn were Mark H. and Lee N.—broke into guffaws for no apparent reason. "Is it something I've done that they're laughing at?" wondered Janet, feeling her face burn.

The class looked pretty bad to Janet. She saw none of the kids she hung around with. The class was full of people she knew were the school troublemakers, and a lot of kind of dumb kids. And there was Susan N., already arguing vociferously with someone. "I'll never get up my nerve to talk in this class," Janet decided. She feigned intense interest in her world history textbook while waiting for Mr. Stanford to start the class.

CHARACTERISTICS OF THE ORIENTATION STAGE

Like Janet, most persons entering a new group experience anxiety and uncertainty. They seek answers to three kinds of basic questions:

1. What is going to happen here? What will this experience be like?

Although they may be too timid to ask, students in a new class have a myriad of questions—about course requirements, the grading system, the teacher's methods, whether the teacher is "hard" or "easy," the content of the course. They watch the teacher closely for nonverbal as well as verbal clues that will tell them something about the teacher's expectations. Students look for reassurance that the new experience will be something they can handle and that it will not hurt them in any way. Of course, what one student can handle, another may find terribly threatening. Janet, for example, was reluctant to speak in front of groups; but Susan N. thoroughly enjoyed class discussion of controversial issues. It's not possible to allay every student's fears completely, but the more information the teacher can give the class about what will be happening to them, the more their initial anxiety will dissipate.

2. Who are the other people here? What are they like?

Immediately upon entering a new classroom, students look around the room, as Janet did, to find out who makes up the new group. They hope to find at least a few persons they already know with whom they can ally themselves, and they try to spot potential sources of conflict or threat. Janet, for example, scanned the group and spotted Shari as the only person she knew well enough to sit beside, and she was simultaneously aware of possible problems with Mike, Susan, Lee, and Mark. In an entry in her personal journal made on that first day of class, Janet wrote:

> The one thing that will keep me from adding to class discussions is Susan N. She is on the debate team and will argue just to argue a point whether she is right or not. She can talk you out of almost anything. I know whatever I say she'll disagree with it.

The process of finding out what others in the class are like continues during the succeeding days and weeks as the students slowly become more familiar with each other. The degree to which they become acquainted depends not only on the social skills of each student, but on what the teacher chooses to do. Many teachers leave the getting acquainted process entirely to chance, and often many students spend month after month in a class not even knowing the names of most of their classmates. Once, when substituting for a fellow teacher toward the end of the semester, I was curious about why many of the students in the class did not refer to one another by name. I found that the vast majority of them didn't know each other. "It's like that in all my classes," one student told me. I asked her how she would go about finding out a classmate's name if she had to know it. She answered, "I'd casually pick up one of his textbooks and flip open the cover to see what name was written there." I marveled silently at her indirectness and speculated about the ludicrous situation that might result if the classmate happened to have borrowed a friend's textbook that day!

To develop a group identity and become a productive group, members need to learn about each other as quickly as possible. The teacher should provide deliberate opportunities and activities for students to learn each other's names as soon as possible and to find out what the other class members are like.

3. Where do I fit in with these people? How will I be treated here?

One reason students are so interested in finding out what the other members of the class are like is that this information may help answer the third concern they have: Will the people here like me and treat me kindly, or will they dislike and hurt me? Janet was dismayed to find that the class contained many "troublemakers" and "dumb kids" because these were people she had usually not been comfortable with. Perhaps their own discomfort caused them to make fun of her for being a cooperative, successful student. Janet interpreted the laughter from Mark and Lee as evidence that she was likely to face ridicule or rejection in this class; she anticipated that Susan would discourage her from participating in class activities and would not show interest in what Janet had to say.

Unfortunately, like many of us, Janet is aware of the impact of others on her, but not of her impact on them. Janet was unaware that her own shyness caused other people (Shari, for example) to think she wasn't interested in them. They considered her aloof and were afraid to approach her. They thus confirmed her worst fears that they wouldn't accept her. And a vicious cycle is put into motion.

What is needed is for members of a group to talk as openly as they can about how it feels to be with a new group of persons, and about what response they would like to get from the group. The teacher concerned about group development can help a great deal by providing opportunities for the class to confront directly this issue of acceptance by the group, thus minimizing misunderstandings that keep people from ever getting to know and trust each other.

HELPFUL TEACHER BEHAVIOR IN THE ORIENTATION STAGE

The activities a teacher plans for the first days of class should be based directly on the needs of students to know what is going to happen in the class, to know who the other people are, and to know how they will be treated in this new group.

Explain what students can expect will happen in your class.

Open the class with a clear explanation of content, requirements, and procedures for the course. Tell students about the kinds of subject matter they will be encountering, what you expect of them in academic work and classroom behavior, your grading system. Give students ample time to ask questions, and answer them patiently even if it requires you to repeat things you just finished announcing. Remember that these questions arise from anxiety which has kept students from receiving messages clearly.

Answer all questions raised by students immediately, however petty or inappropriate they may seem. Do not postpone an explanation ("I'll explain grades after the first test," or "Why don't you hold that question until I've issued the textbooks?"). Try to sense what feelings prompted the student to ask the question and respond to those feelings.

Help students get acquainted with you and with one another.

Include in your introduction to the course a brief description of yourself. Be sure to mention non-school-related aspects, such as hobbies, family background, names and ages of spouse and children, that will reveal to the class that you are a live human being, not just a phantom who disappears into the chalkbox after school. You will also be providing many structured getting-acquainted experiences (see the section that follows) through which members of the group can learn about one another, and you should participate in those activities in order to allow the group to learn more about you.

Be a model of the behavior you expect.

Through your own behavior and the way you structure the class, you are providing students with clues about how they will be treated in your classroom and how you expect them to treat each other. For example, your actions will convey whether, and on what basis, discrimination and lack of acceptance are going to be norms in the group. It is not so much what you say but what you do that tells students whether you treat black students differently from white students, sloppily dressed students differently from neat ones, boys differently from girls, attractive students differently from homely ones, bright students differently from slower ones.

Your students will be watching your behavior very carefully to determine whether it is safe to be themselves in your class, or whether they are going to be rejected for any reason. Few of us would deliberately and overtly reject a student, but most of us are guilty of subtle discrimination. Members of Janet's class, for example, accused me of favoring boys over girls, pointing out that I talked to boys in the class far more than I did to girls. Students are very adept at reading nonverbal clues, and easily pick up the message that certain kinds of students are treated better than others, even when the teacher is unconscious of it. For example, we all tend to stand physically closer to and make more physical contacts with people we like best.

Never put down, embarrass, ridicule, tease, or laugh at a student, and if one student does this to another, act swiftly to squelch it. State firmly to the offender, "That remark was a putdown and that kind of talk is not acceptable in my class. I feel hurt when people make fun of me." Letting the offender know where you stand establishes a norm against ridicule and conveys to the victims of the attack (and potential victims of other attacks) that you are willing to support them. It also demonstrates the norm of open communication. Some teachers wonder, "Doesn't it add to the victim's embarrassment for the teacher to make a big deal about it in front of the class?" This may be so for groups who are not used to communicating directly. Actually, the victim probably feels more hurt by the demeaning remark than embarrassed by your pointing out that such an attack is offensive and unacceptable in your class. Supporting the victim reinforces the kind of behavior you want to establish as a norm.

The physical structure of the classroom can also

provide answers to the question, "How will I be treated here?" Arranging chairs in a circle indicates that all students are of equal importance and are worthy of being seen and heard. Using random selection when assigning students to small groups indicates that they will be treated democratically and their contributions valued equally.

The way you deal with new members entering the class is crucial. They have the same orientation needs as the other students. Failing to provide them with the information they missed conveys to the rest of the group that you do not consider the needs and rights of all members equally valid, and it retards the new students' integration into the class.

During the Orientation Stage, it is essential that you continually monitor yourself to be sure that your personal behavior is consistent with your goals for the group. For instance, if you expect students to develop openness and honesty in their communication within the group, you yourself must answer questions—even awkward ones—with candor. Complete consistency between goals and behavior is, of course, never possible. Few of us ever thoroughly practice what we preach. But to the degree that we can become aware of both our verbal and non-verbal behavior we can narrow the gap between our actions and the principles we espouse for our students.

STRUCTURED EXPERIENCES FOR THE ORIENTATION STAGE

The first step in meeting students' needs for information about the other members of the group is learning everybody's name. Procedures such as the following can make name learning faster, easier, and more fun. One or two activities can be used each day during the first week.

Naming Exercises.

1.   Name Tags.   Give each student a 4″ x 6″ index card and a crayon or felt-tip marker. Instruct students to print in big letters on the card the name they would like to be called in the group. In the upper right hand corner, have them write two adjectives to describe themselves (curious, vivacious, sincere, athletic, etc.). In the upper left hand corner, they write several words ending in -ing that tell things they enjoy doing (boating, reading, sleeping, swimming, etc.). At the bottom of the card they write the name of a place they'd like to visit; or any other information you might think appropriate for your group, such as the name of a favorite character from a movie, a book, or TV; or something they have that they're proud of; or something they're good at; or what they'd buy with $50; or something they enjoyed doing during the summer.

Have them put on their tags with masking tape or a pin and mill around the room looking at each other's tags. Suggest that they not talk at all while inspecting other people's name tags. Students may continue to wear their tags in the classroom during the first few days.

If students feel name tags are too childish (I've had several classes that did), try having them make name plates for their desks (such as business executives display) out of heavy paper folded into an inverted V.

2.   Self-Introductions.   Have students come up one at a time and write their names on the chalkboard. They then tell the group anything about themselves that would help the group get to know them better. Everybody in the class takes out a sheet of paper and writes down each person's name and also jots down next to each name something that will serve as a reminder of that person.

Even though you may have introduced yourself to the class previously, *you* should begin this activity. Walk to the board, write your name—first and surname—turn to the class and say something like, "I'm Jerry Haritatos. My real first name was a long and complicated Greek name that nobody could ever pronounce, so I changed it legally several years ago. I have taught Social Studies here at King Junior High for three years. Before that I was in the Peace Corps in Ethiopia. My hobbies are gardening and playing tennis and taking home movies of my three-year-old daughter, Amy."

Then start on one side of the room and have the students come to the board one at a time and introduce themselves. Go around the class systematically rather than waiting for volunteers. If students have trouble knowing what to say about themselves, suggest they mention hobbies, interests, brothers and sisters, how they spend after-school time. Do not allow other students to ask questions; the speakers themselves should be allowed to decide how much they want to reveal. After all students have introduced themselves, suggest that they keep the lists they have made as a reminder.

Concerning this activity, Janet wrote in her journal:

> *Today the activities in our class were very unusual. To start, each person in the class, including Mr. Stanford, introduced himself to the class and told things about himself. . . . It was kind of embarrassing to talk about ourselves.*

3. Who Are Your Neighbors? For this get-acquainted game, seat students in a large circle. The teacher may be the first "It," or a student can volunteer. "It" stands in the middle of the circle (without a chair). Instruct all players to learn the names of the persons seated on either side of them. Then "It" walks up to any player and asks, "Who are your neighbors?" The player who doesn't answer correctly automatically becomes "It." The former "It" takes the new "It's" place, learning the neighbor's names, and the game proceeds.

If the player answers correctly, "It" asks, "Do you want new neighbors?"

If the player answers *yes*, the entire group must change seats, with "It" scrambling for a seat, leaving someone standing as the new "It."

If the player answers *no*, "It" asks, "Who should have new neighbors?" The player gives the names of any two members of the group. The two players named must exchange places while "It" tries to take one of their seats, leaving one of them standing as the new "It."

Whenever places are changed, the students should learn the names of their new neighbors, and then continue playing the next round.

4.   Name Chain.   Seat the group in one large circle; you should sit in the circle as part of the group. Give the following instructions: "We've spent a couple of days telling each other our names. Now let's test ourselves. I'll start by telling my name." Say to the person on your left, "You repeat my name and add your own name. We will continue around the circle, going clockwise. When it is your turn, repeat all the names of all those who preceded you, and add your own name. If you forget someone's name, ask that person to repeat it for you."

This activity, although rather mechanical, is probably the fastest way to teach a group one another's names. It has the added benefit of requiring every person in the group to speak, and to look at all the other members, thus getting students comfortable with student-to-student participation in discussion.

5.   Name Quick Draw.   Push the desks against the wall or find a large open space in which the group can move around freely. Give these instructions: "I want you to mill around this space at random without talking, but looking directly at the other members of the group as you pass them. Imagine that you are Western gunfighters out looking for a duel. As soon as you make eye contact with another gunfighter, quickly pantomime drawing a revolver and 'shoot' the other person by calling out that person's name loudly. The one who is first to call the other's name correctly wins the duel. The other drops to the floor 'dead' or staggers out of the game. The gunfighter who stays alive longest is the winner."

After the group has played for a while, point out that a number of persons didn't wait until they made eye contact before "shooting." (Students will frequently charge up behind someone and scream the person's name, allowing the other person no chance to draw.) Suggest that they all "come back to life" and play another round, this time being more careful about eye contact.

6. Adjective Alliteration. Go around the circle and have students state their names, preceded with an adjective. The adjective should start with the same initial sound as the person's name and should describe some positive quality (for example, "Generous Gene"). The word might be an -ing word that tells of something the person does well, or it might be just a descriptive adjective.

Getting-Acquainted Exercises.

The next step in helping students find out who the members of the group are is to provide opportunities for members to share information about themselves. This increases the amount of trust in the group because it helps students to know better what to expect from one another. Also, group members may discover that they have many things in common and may become more comfortable with each other. This sharing of information has already begun in the name activities suggested above. But the process has only barely begun, and the activities suggested below should be used during the early days and weeks of a group's life together in order to move its members smoothly through the Orientation Stage. Not every one of the activities must be used, of course, but the more activities a group experiences, the more likely it is that members will have their orientation needs met and will be able to "grow" on to the next stage of development.

All of the activities designed to promote getting acquainted involve some degree of *self-disclosure*, the revealing of personal information about oneself to others. Most of us are not comfortable revealing things about ourselves to a person we barely know. There are things about ourselves that we think other people might laugh at, or ridicule, or that might cause people to dislike us if they knew about them. In psychological terminology, these things are *threatening*—we think that something bad may happen to us if we tell someone about them. For example, most of us are reluctant to tell a new acquaintance about a talent we have for fear that the person will think we are bragging. A young woman is unlikely to admit that she enjoys looking at male nudes in magazines, not just because this is personal, but because she is afraid of the reaction of other people when she tells them.

Therefore, for most of us, self-disclosure is a gradual process. Like easing slowly into cold water, we move in stages, telling a new person more and more about ourselves as time goes on, always alert (whether we're conscious of it or not) for the reaction. If the reaction is favorable, we tend to reveal more. We, in effect, *trust* the person with more significant details about ourselves.

This process of opening up or, to put it more technically, decreasing our anxiety about self-disclosure, usually takes many months or years if it is left to chance. We have to go through many, many experiences of first sharing insignificant, superficial things about ourselves, and then sharing more and more threatening things, always monitoring the other person's reaction to make sure we won't be hurt because we've revealed too much of ourselves. In many situations, we avoid talking about things of personal significance, because of our anxiety about self-disclosure. Most school situations follow this pattern. Students are rarely given the opportunity to build up the trust that will enable them to share personal information with one another. So, if the teacher ever does ask a question that requires a personal response (such as "Have you ever been lonely?"), the question is so threatening that students can't handle it.

Most educators agree that education should be relevant to the life of the student. For students to make connections between school subjects and their own lives, they need opportunities to talk with each other about their lives. This process requires greater self-disclosure than usually takes place in school. It is essential that we prepare students for this higher level of self-disclosure. To reduce students' anxiety and speed up the process of opening up, we can structure activities that start students at a superficial level of self-disclosure, and move them to deeper levels gradually enough that they do not become threatened, but much faster than would occur if the process were left to chance.

The getting-acquainted exercises suggested below can be used to bring about this increased depth of self-disclosure. In choosing which activities to use, how to use them, and in which order, the following principles may be kept in mind.

First, the sequence of activities should begin at a level of self-disclosure that is not at all threatening and should move to deeper levels at a rate so gradual that students do not become anxious. Two factors determine how threatening an activity is: *what* the student is asked to say, and *to whom*;—that is, the *content* and the *structure* of the activity.

The content of an activity is more threatening the closer it is to the "inside" of the person. To ask students how they would spend $50 if it were given to them is less threatening than to ask them how they feel about their mothers. A question is threatening to the degree that people fear that others might dislike them (or otherwise reject them) depending on how they answer it. Questions that deal with our values, feelings, and opinions are potentially threatening and have to be approached gradually and cautiously.

An activity whose structure requires the individual to talk to a large number of people is more threatening than an activity structured for small groups. It's easier for most of us to talk about ourselves to one person, or to a small group, than to an entire class of 30 persons. It's easier to talk to people we know and like than to strangers. It's also easier to reveal ourselves to others who have been revealing themselves to us. It is more threatening if the teacher singles out a student to call on, or asks students to volunteer, than if the teacher goes around the circle, having each student answer the same question (e.g. "When was the last time you felt lonely?"). Likewise, students will find an activity less threatening if the teacher also participates—especially if the teacher starts off the activity to demonstrate that it's not such a frightening thing to talk about after all. Finally, the threat level of any activity can be lessened by assuring students that it's perfectly all right to "pass" if they do not want to answer a question or to participate in an exercise.

In planning a series of getting-acquainted/self-disclosure activities, you can choose the content and structure that are appropriate in order to move your particular class gradually into deeper levels. The content of many of the activities can be infinitely altered, depending on how much threat the group can tolerate. For example, in the *Double Circles* activity below, in which the students talk to only one other person at a time and change partners regularly, the topic the students are to talk about can vary from how tall they are to how they felt about the death of a fellow student, depending on how much self-disclosure the group is comfortable with.

The *Forced Choice* activity is generally a low-threat activity because its structure requires students to indicate their opinions simply by moving to some part of the room without explaining their choice to anyone. But if the *content* for the *Forced Choice* is high-threat (e.g. "Would you engage in premarital sex?"), the activity obviously requires a high level of self-disclosure and should come much later.

Round Robin generally is a high-threat activity, since it requires that every student talk to the entire class, but with low-threat content (e.g. "Do you have any pets?"). This activity could easily be used early in the sequence.

Therefore, it's not necessary to adhere to the order in which the activities are presented below. The content and/or structure can be altered to make the activities appropriate at different places in the self-disclosure hierarchy. You must simply watch the group closely to see how they are reacting to various structures and contents and be prepared to alter them accordingly. When students begin to giggle more than usual, or become hostile, or engage in horseplay and other disruptive behavior, it's likely that you're moving too fast for them, and you should shift to a topic or a structure that is less threatening.

Self-disclosure activities can often be designed to utilize the content of the course. For example, in the *Double Circles* activity students could be instructed to "Tell your partners which character in the novel we've read you liked best and why" (low-threat question), or "Tell your partners which character in the novel you are most similar to and why" (higher-threat question). *Forced Choice* could be utilized to see how students stand on social issues. A question such as "Should all pesticides be banned because of their harmful effects on the environment?" could be used in biology class with the *Voting Questions* structure.

1. Who's-in-the-Group. Each student and the teacher complete a form similar to the one below. Instruct everyone to find people in the class who fit each category and obtain their signatures in the space provided. Suggest or require that no name be used more than once. After everybody has finished, seat the class in a circle and ask: Which items was it difficult to get a signature for? What have you learned about various people in the class that you didn't know before? Did you discover anything that surprised you?

WHO'S-IN-THE-GROUP FORM

1. A person in this group who has never been outside our state is _____.

2. A person in this group whose first name starts with the same letter as mine is _____.

3. A person in this group who likes the same sports I do is _____.

4. A person in this group who was born outside our state is _____.

5. A person in this group whose hair is the same color as mine is _____.

6. A person in this group whose eyes are the same color as mine is _____.

7. A person in this group who has read the same book that I have read is _____.

8. A person in this group who is shorter than I am is _____.

9. A person in this group whose birthday falls in the same month as mine is _____.

10. A person in this group who wears the same size shoes that I do is _____.

11. A person in this group who is taller than I am is _____.

12. A person in this group who has the same hobby as I is _____.

13. A person in this group who likes the same TV program as I is _____.

14. A person in this group who likes school is _____.

15. A person in this group who does not have a middle name is _____.

16. A person in this group who owns a horse is _____.

17. A person in this group who has traveled outside the U.S. is _____.

18. A person in this group whom I would like to get better acquainted with is _____.

19. A person in this group whose last name starts with the same letter as mine is _____.

20. A person in this group who has lived in the same house all of his/her life is _____.

21. A person in this group who has the same number of brothers and sisters as I is _____.

22. A person in this group who likes math better than English is _____.

23. A person in this group whose favorite color is red is _____.

24. A person in this group whose favorite color is the same as mine is _____.

25. A person in this group whom I liked immediately upon first meeting is _____.

2. Interview and Introduce. Instruct each student to find someone in the group who is relatively unknown. Have the partners interview each other, attempting to get to know each other. You might introduce some structure by suggesting, for example, that they learn five things about each other that they couldn't tell by just looking, or that they find out what their partner enjoys doing outside of school. After about ten minutes have the partners introduce each other to the group telling what they learned about each other.

3. Art Projects. Have students construct one of the following and explain it to some one person (lower-threat) or the whole group (higher-threat):

> a) A *trademark* for themselves, drawn or painted on heavy paper with colored pencils, crayons, or felt-tip markers.

> b) A *collage* that illustrates various aspects of themselves, made from pictures clipped from magazines and selected objects pasted onto paper.

> c) A *coat of arms* in which various aspects of themselves are drawn on a shield-shaped piece of heavy paper divided into sections. Each section might be assigned to represent a particular thing—greatest accomplishment, personal quality most proud of, hobby or interest, goals, distinguishing physical characteristics—to be represented by a drawing, design, picture, or symbol.

4. I Am . . . List. Arrange the group in a circle and sit with them as a member of the group. Give each person a sheet of paper numbered from one to ten down the left hand side, with about one inch between numbers. After each number are the words *I am.*

Instruct the group as follows: "I'd like each of us—working alone—to complete each of these statements, by writing after each 'I am' a word or phrase that tells something about ourselves. For example, you might wish to say 'the oldest child in my family' or 'the owner of an Afghan hound' or 'the kind of person who doesn't like to go to bed early,' or anything else that would tell the class something we don't know about you."

After you and the students have finished your lists, proceed in order around the circle—starting with yourself—having everybody read one of the sentences on their list. Continue in the same way with other sentences until all responses have been read. For lower threat, have students meet in small groups or dyads (pairs) to share the information on their lists.

5. Double Circles.   Ask students to push back their desks to create a large empty space in the middle of the room. Divide the class into two groups by having members number off "one, two, one, two," etc. Then have all the "ones" stand in a circle facing out. The "twos" form a larger circle outside the "ones," with each "two" facing a "one." If the class has an odd number of students in it, you will need to participate as well as giving the following directions: "Do you know the name of your partner? If not, find out. (Pause.) Now, each of you tell your partner what you would buy if you had $50 to spend. (Pause.) Now I want the people in the outer circle to move one step to the right so they are facing a new partner."

Continue using the same procedure, checking names and answering different questions until the students are back to their original partners. Use questions such as the following, arranging them in order from lower-threat to higher-threat:

> If you had to change your first name, what would the new one be?
>
> Who is your heroine or hero and why?

What subject in school are you best at?

If you could spend an hour talking to some famous person, who would it be?

What is one thing that makes you happy?

What is your favorite TV program (food, musical group, pastime, color, season, etc.)?

If you had to live somewhere else for a year, where would it be?

What is one thing you like about school and one thing you dislike?

What is something you like about yourself? (high-threat)

What is your greatest strength or greatest accomplishment? (high-threat)

What one thing about yourself would you change? (high-threat)

You may also use subject-matter related questions to introduce a topic you will be working on and have members get acquainted at the same time. For example, suppose you were going to begin a unit on culture and change, you might use the following questions in the *Double Circles* format:

Describe the place where you lived when you were five years old.

In what ways do you think you are typical of the citizens of the town you live in?

In what ways do you think you are not typical of the citizens of the town you live in?

If you had to move to Saudi Arabia next year, what would you miss most about the place where you now live?

What one change would you most like to see in our society?

What change has occurred in our society during your lifetime that you like the most?

What change has occurred in our society during your lifetime that you like the least?

6. Voting Questions.[1] Seat the class in a circle. Ask a series of questions that begin with "How many of you. . ?" After each question, have students indicate their positions as follows:

Yes, very much—raise hands and wave them around

Yes, moderately—raise hands

Undecided, don't want to say—sit with arms folded

No, moderately—thumbs down

No, very much—thumbs down, moving hands back and forth rapidly

Questions can deal with anything students might have feelings about, or they may deal with subject-matter issues that students have an opinion on. For example:

How many of you have been so angry in the last week that you wanted to hit someone?

How many of you think you might like to join the Peace Corps?

How many of you think it's wrong to shoplift?

---

[1]"Voting Questions" and the two activities that follow it are adapted from *Values Clarification*, by Sidney B. Simon, Leland W. Howe, and Howard Kirschenbaum, New York: Hart Publishing Co., 1972.

How many of you feel it's good to have friends of another race or ethnic group?

How many of you would give your life for something you believe in?

How many of you think the purpose of the Civil War was to free the slaves?

How many of you think the U.S. should give large amounts of food to starving nations?

A recent government study showed that schools are not doing enough to eliminate race and sex discrimination. How many of you agree?

In *The Cat Ate My Gym Suit* Mrs. Lewis had to decide whether to obey her husband or do what she thought was right. How many of you think a woman should do what her husband tells her?

In *We Are But a Moment's Sunlight* the authors point out that funeral services can fill the emotional needs of the survivors. How many of you would want to go to the funeral if your friend died?

Instruct the group to keep their hands up (or down) long enough for everyone to look around and see how everyone else is voting. As with other self-disclosure activities, the questions should begin with less threatening ones and gradually progress to more threatening ones. This activity makes an excellent introduction to a subject-matter lesson if the questions allow the students to express their opinions on issues related to the content of the lesson. After all the questions have been asked, a group discussion may take place on one or more of the questions. A particularly good choice would be one on which there was wide disagreement. You may hold an open discussion with the entire group, or you may break the class into small groups, each with a representative cross-section of opinion.

7. Forced Choice.   Have the class move back their desks so that a large empty space is created. Then ask a question that requires students to make an either-or decision (such as, "Which would you rather visit, Europe or Africa?"). Instruct all students who take one position to move to one side of the room and all those who take the other position to move to the opposite side. Do not allow anyone to "straddle the fence," pointing out that we frequently face decisions in life in which neither alternative seems better than the other. When students have voted by moving to the appropriate side of the room, have them look around to see how others have voted. As a variation, you might instruct students to find a partner among those persons on their own side of the room and discuss briefly why they made the choice they did.

Questions can deal with opinions and personal qualities, or can be related to subject-matter issues. For example:

If you had a choice between a job in a big city with bad air pollution or one in a rural area where the nearest town was 40 miles away, which would you choose?

Would you rather watch TV or go to a movie?

Which would you rather be, president of Ford Motor Company or a U.S. senator?

Do you like to spend your time with lots of people around or are you happier alone?

Would you rather attend a symphony concert or a boxing match?

Are you a leader or a follower?

Would you have fought for the Arabs or the Israelis in the 1973 War?

Which can you tolerate better, a classroom that is 10° too hot, or one that is 10° too cold?

Would you rather be a drug addict or a practicing homosexual?

If your girlfriend were pregnant, would you rather she have an abortion or give the baby up for adoption?

8. Continuum. Have the class move back their desks to create a large empty space. Ask a question or present an issue that offers many shades of opinion and alternative positions. Designate one side of the room as representing one extreme, and the opposite side as the other extreme. Tell students to imagine that a line is drawn from one side to the other, and have them place themselves on that line according to their position on the issue. For example, suppose the question is, "Should the United States sell wheat to foreign countries even if it causes food prices to rise at home?" One wall of the classroom might represent "Yes, always" and the opposite wall might represent "Never," with the middle floor space designating various positions in between.

After all members have lined themselves up on the continuum, have them look around to see the range of opinion that exists in the group. You can then have the students take their seats and conduct a total-class discussion on the issue they have just examined by way of the continuum. Or you can move on to another issue and have students rearrange themselves on the continuum according to their opinions. Often it is helpful to have the class do several continuums in order to see that, depending on the issue, their classmates fall at different positions on the continuum.

9. Secondhand Description. Have students choose a partner (low-threat), or conduct the activity with the entire group seated in a circle (higher-threat). Instruct students to think of a person who knows them very well—a family member, a close friend, a relative, a teacher. Then have them describe themselves as they think that person would describe them. For instance, here is Andy describing himself as he thinks his brother Jeff might describe him: "My brother Andy is a kinda neat guy—he wins all sorts of awards for model airplanes that he builds, and he has a terrific collection of snakes and other reptiles. But sometimes he does things that I don't like, such as making me mow the lawn when he has things he wants to do. In general, though, I think Andy's an all right guy."

10. Sentence Stems. Duplicate a list of sentence stems, such as the following, and give a copy to each student to complete in writing. Answers can be shared with a partner, a small group, or the entire class.

a) I like . . .

b) Sometimes I wish . . .

c) Whenever I make a poor grade . . .

d) I can't . . .

e) When I was younger . . .

f) Most people I know . . .

g) I need to know . . .

h) Whenever I enter a new group . . .

i) I regret . . .

j) My goal . . .

k) I'm afraid . . .

l) It makes me proud when I . . .

m) A good thing that happened recently was . . .

11.   Magic Shop.   Seat the class in a circle and give the following instructions. "I want you to imagine that I am the proprietor of a Magic Shop—a place where you can exchange a personal characteristic you have but don't like for one that you'd rather have. For example, you can offer to trade me your tendency to talk about people behind their backs for the ability to control your temper." Go around the circle, giving every student a chance to make a trade in the shop. Do not allow questions or discussion until all students have had an opportunity to respond.

12.   Acting Out.   Have students take turns pantomiming a personal quality or a hobby, talent, or interest, and have the group try to guess what it is.

13.   Round Robin.   Seat the class in a circle. Ask a question such as those for *Double Circles* on page 62 and, beginning with yourself, go around the circle giving every student an opportunity to answer. Do not let the other students react or ask questions until everyone has answered. Students who do not want to answer may "pass" gracefully. Questions may be low- or high-threat and can deal with personal information or with subject-matter issues. For a class that is ready for higher-threat questions, try the following:

> What is one thing that other people like about you?
>
> On what occasion were your feelings hurt? (or were you afraid, or happy, or proud, or angry, or worried, etc.)
>
> When you are in a new group, when do you feel most comfortable?
>
> How are you different from most people your age?
>
> What do you value most?
>
> What will you be like ten years from now?

How have you changed most since last year?

What is something you usually don't like to talk about?

Who in this group are you most similar to?

Who in this group likes you best?

Who in this group can influence you most?

What's one thing it takes courage for you to do?

What do you like best about yourself?

After everyone has had a chance to respond to one question, you may wish to conduct a total-class discussion of the question, allowing all students to share their ideas in random order. Or, if you simply want students to see the spectrum of opinion in the class, you may wish to go around the circle again with new questions.

14. Visiting Celebrity. Explain to the class that you will be playing a game similar to "Meet the Press" or "Face the Nation." Ask for a volunteer to be the person interviewed and tell the rest of the class they are the "reporters." They are to take turns asking questions to find out what kind of person the interviewee is, but make it clear that the interviewee has the option of responding to any question with "no comment."

Concerning this activity, Janet wrote in her journal:

Today we played a new "game," as our class called it. We focused on one person at a time and asked any question we wanted. He had the alternative to say "no comment" if he didn't want to answer. When I was focused on, I had the most fun. I liked being the center of attention. When I had to ask the question, I didn't know what to ask. The kids I knew well, I didn't have anything to ask. With those I didn't know well, I felt kind of nosey. The only person in the class whose answers surprised me was Mr. Stanford. I thought that he was happier teaching English than he is. I had no idea that he'd be leaving after this year. Actually, today's class was really fun. I like the "experimental English" better than regular English, because we try new things that take thought but the end result is worth it!

15.   Tell It Like It Is: The Ungame.[2]   This commercial game-that-isn't-a-game provides a fun means of getting better acquainted. Players roll die and move around the board answering questions on cards. Most questions are nonthreatening (e.g. "What is your favorite food?" "Name two famous people you'd like to have for parents.") and even the more serious ones (e.g. "When was the last time you cried? Why?") are appropriate for classroom sharing. Up to six students can play. (A special Group Pak accommodates 30 persons.) The game requires no supervision or teacher direction; rules are simple and easily understood by even young children. One of these games could be kept on a shelf in the classroom for use by a small group of students when they've finished other work early, or as part of a deliberate getting-acquainted program during the Orientation Stage.

Trust-Building Exercises.

To deal with the third concern students have during the Orientation Stage, "How will I be treated here?", it is helpful to let students talk about how they see themselves fitting into the group; how they imagine the group will react to them; and how they would like to be treated by the group. Activities such as

---

[2]"Tell It Like It Is: The Ungame" is available from Au-Vid Incorporated, P.O. Box 964, Garden Grove, California 92642.

the following can act as springboards to discussion of these issues.

1. Seeking Allies. Go around the circle, asking students in turn to name another member of the group they think they are most similar to. This is a fairly high-threat activity. If the class has become very cohesive and the trust level is high, it may be possible to ask students to explain how they are similar to the other person. Otherwise, have them merely say the person's name.

2. Imagining Reactions. Arrange the group in a circle and sit with the group like any other member. Tell the students, "I want you to think of your deepest, darkest, innermost secret, the last thing that you would ever tell to the people here. I will not ask you to tell that secret or in any way reveal it, so don't be worried. I only want you to think about that secret in your own mind. (Pause.) Has every one thought of a secret? Good. Now I want you to imagine, simply imagine, that you had just told that secret right here, right now, to this group. What do you think the reaction of the people in this group would be? Would they laugh? Would they be understanding? Would they be sad? Would they dislike you? Would they be horrified and never speak to you again? Just how do you think they would react? Can you imagine the expression on their faces if you told your secret? What would they say to you? How would they treat you after class?" Ask for volunteers to describe what they imagine the reaction of the class would be if they told their secret.

3. Performance.[3] Give each student a copy of the following list:

---

[3] "Performance" is adapted from *Self-Awareness Through Group Dynamics*, by Richard Reichert, Dayton, Ohio: Pflaum/Standard, 1970. Used with permission of the publisher.

Imitate the crowing of a rooster.

Give a two-minute talk about your best qualities.

Do a silent pantomime of a very sleepy person washing in the morning.

Give a two-minute talk on what you like most about your classmates.

Recite a short nursery rhyme you remember from your childhood.

Balance a book on your head and walk across the room.

Choose a short passage from any book in the classroom to read aloud. Tell the students, "I want you to number the activities on the list from one to seven, in the order that you would most prefer doing them in front of the group. Number the activity you would most prefer *one*, and the activity you would least prefer *seven*. Any one of you may be called upon to actually perform one of your first three choices, so you should give serious thought to how you mark your preferences."

When everyone has finished marking the list, ask by a show of hands how many rated the first item as number one on their list. Do the same with each item, recording the results. Then ask students to comment on why they think certain items were chosen as number one more often than others.

Continue the discussion with questions such as the following:

Did you feel uneasy about the whole idea of possibly having to perform one of the items on the list?

In what way do you think your ordering of the list reflects how much you trust the others in the group?

Is it harder for you to do something silly in a group (such as imitating a rooster) or to do something serious (like talk about your own good qualities)?

Why is it important for us to be able to trust the others in this group?

What can we do in this class to make it easier for us to do things that are normally hard or embarrassing?

4. Ideal Reactions. Go around the circle and have each person answer this question: "What could the people in the group do to make you feel more free to talk in front of them about things that are important to you?" Try to get students to describe specific behavior that makes them feel more comfortable, such as listening carefully, not laughing, asking questions, smiling sympathetically.

Before the group goes on to the Norm Establishment Stage, members should be comfortable with each other. This will take a different amount of time with different groups. You may use some or all of the activities described here, or make up similar activities to achieve the desired goal of more open communication and greater trust within the group.

3 STAGE TWO: ESTABLISHING NORMS GOAL ONE: GROUP RESPONSIBILITY

"You don't know anything about blacks!" shouted Susan. "You're just prejudiced."

"You always think you're so smart!" Jay yelled back. "The only black you ever knew was your mother's cleaning lady!"

Janet shrank back in her chair. "Why doesn't Mr. Stanford stop them?" she wondered. "Can't he see that this discussion is getting out of hand? Why doesn't he just shut Susan up and explain the story himself?"

More voices were joining the fray, but Janet tuned them out. She stared at the short story they had been reading, wishing she could blot out the discordant voices around her and maybe do the study questions about the story instead. "This discussion is really boring," she thought.

Susan, however, was having a great time. She felt that she had just demonstrated conclusively that St. Louis' segregation patterns were worse than New York City's. She gloated as she looked around the room. "This is going to be a great class!" she thought.

But Lee didn't share her enthusiasm. For him it was like

countless other discussions he'd endured in past years. "Seems like only Susan and her loud-mouthed friends care about this," he thought. He sometimes thought he might like to join in, but there was rarely a chance—and, anyway, he hadn't read the assignment. So he sat back and watched with a smile as Jay and his friends continued their shouting match with Susan.

"Can anyone now see the relationship between the segregation patterns in the city and the problems of the main character?" asked Mr. Stanford, his voice reflecting his annoyance that the discussion had strayed so far from the topic.

"Segregation may be bad, but it's nothing compared to the treatment the Jews received in Germany," announced Jay.

"That may be true," Mr. Stanford said, on the verge of losing his temper. "But we are trying to discuss this story by James Baldwin. . . ."

"But this is important—" interrupted Jay. He launched into a brilliant description of the gory details of Auschwitz, loud enough and fast enough that Susan couldn't get a word in edgewise.

"Why doesn't Mr. Stanford do something?" thought Janet. Bruce was drawing a dirty picture and passing it to a couple of his friends. Lee saw it and motioned for them to pass it down to him.

Most of the class sat as silently as Janet, probably as bored as she was. "This is a stupid story anyway," thought Janet. "But maybe now that Mr. Stanford sees how bad discussions are he'll lecture instead—or at least let us write answers to study questions."

During the previous three weeks Janet's class had become reasonably well acquainted. They now felt freer with one another and less inhibited. But they were far from being a productive group. For when it came to working together in a discussion or group project, their interaction was chaotic and ineffectual. Now they faced a long and complex struggle to establish procedures that would help them accomplish their goals. The process of establishing these productive ways of interacting takes place in the Norm Establishment Stage.

CHARACTERISTICS OF THE
NORM ESTABLISHMENT STAGE

The Norm Establishment Stage is crucial in a group's growth toward maturity. It is the period during which members learn to organize themselves into an effective team. They struggle with issues of power—who will initiate new ideas, who will get the group organized, who will determine what direction the group will take, who, in short, will furnish leadership. They deal also with the issues of who is important to the work of the group, who gets listened to, who is ignored. The responsibilities of group members are defined during this stage and members learn what kinds of behavior are rewarded by the group. The group must also establish procedures for making decisions and determine to what extent persons with dissenting opinions will be considered.

If the group has completed more or less successfully the getting-acquainted and trust-building exercises of the Orientation Stage, it is likely that cohesiveness in the group is high. When interacting informally, the students should seem to be much more comfortable and less inhibited than the typical class. But at this stage, if they are given a subject-matter task to do together as a group their performance may be poor. Although the getting-acquainted process has been helpful in moving the class toward greater social maturity, being well acquainted isn't enough to assure their success as a working group.

Most people, particularly pre-adolescents and adolescents, have not had opportunities to develop the skills and attitudes that are necessary for productive group work. The norms and procedures that operate in the average classroom are generally antithetical to producing these needed skills and attitudes. For example, in most classes the teacher takes responsibility for everything that happens in the group and fills almost all leadership functions—setting goals, calling on people to contribute, drawing conclusions, and evaluating performance.

In most classes students are expected to interact directly with the teacher most of the time and with other students only occasionally. Hence, when an opportunity does arise for students to work together, most students don't know how to respond to others in a helpful way. They, like Janet's classmates Susan and Jay, mistake heated argument for productive group interaction.

In most classrooms students are taught to compete with one another. Yet, cooperation is required if a group is to function well. Most students don't know how to work cooperatively simply because they've never had a chance to learn.

In most classrooms, problems encountered in group interaction are generally ignored or at best handled by the teacher. If students are to grow up learning how to confront and solve problems, they should begin by coping with real problems in the classroom.

During the Norm Establishment Stage, the teacher must take deliberate steps to inculcate in the group the skills and attitudes needed for effective group work. In order for the group to move on toward maturity, the following norms must be well established:

(1) Group responsibility—Leadership emerges from the group itself; everybody contributes to the work of the group.

(2) Responsiveness to others—Members listen in depth to one another and link together their ideas to build a group product.

(3) Interdependence—Members cooperate to

achieve goals rather than competing with one another.

(4) Decision making through consensus—The groups arrive at decisions satisfactory to all, rather than imposing the will of the majority on the minority.

(5) Confronting problems—Disagreements are faced instead of being ignored, and solutions are sought.

If a group can establish these norms over the first several weeks of its life, it is almost certainly headed for productivity. In this book, a chapter will be devoted to each of these norms in the order in which they are listed above. This seems to be a logical sequence for the teacher to follow in developing these norms. However, the norms are not mutually exclusive, and work on establishing all norms may be going on simultaneously.

HELPFUL TEACHER BEHAVIOR FOR ESTABLISH-ING NORM #1: GROUP RESPONSIBILITY

Although the goal of this developmental stage is for the group to become as self-directing as possible, this does not imply that the teacher relinquishes control of all learning activities and simply sits back and asks the students, "Well, what do you want to do today?"

Two ingredients are necessary if the group is to take responsibility for itself: opportunities to learn the skills needed, and opportunities for the group to practice directing its own activities. The teacher must provide these opportunities. In other words, the teacher must both train the group to assume responsibility, and give its members reasonable amounts of independence to put into action what they have learned. Thus, far from abdicating, the teacher plays a very active role in planning and implementing classroom activities; but it is a new kind of role, and most teachers have not had experience in this role.

The following are suggestions for things the teacher can do to create the kind of classroom structure that encourages students to become self-directing.

Shift from teacher-centered to group-centered learning activities.

In a traditional teacher-centered learning experience the teacher sets all the goals, asks virtually all the questions, calls on students to answer, responds to their answers, keeps the discussion moving in the desired direction, points out relationships between ideas, and draws conclusions. When all I knew was a teacher-centered approach to teaching, I would stand at the front of the room, facing my students who were seated in rows or (if I felt particularly brave) in a double horseshoe. I would have a list of questions I had constructed (or plagiarized) covering the lesson and I'd ask these questions one at a time to stimulate discussion. After each question, I'd stop and look around the room for volunteers. Hands would rise—usually—and I'd select one of these students to answer the question. I would reply to the student's comment in some way, indicating how well the student had done. Often I would expand on the answer, underscoring the important parts and correcting any misconceptions. Or I'd ask if anyone had anything to add to the answer. Sometimes—but rarely—a student might ask a question, but most of the time the students sat quietly (if they were bored and tired) or noisily (if they were bored and restless) until called on.

By contrast, a group-centered learning activity focuses the group's attention on the task it must complete rather than on the teacher standing at the front of the room. Responsibility for completing the task is on the group rather than on the teacher. The group works out some pattern of organization—

sometimes electing a leader, sometimes simply taking turns—
and pools its resources to get the job done. The teacher is
available for consultation, but does not serve as leader. All the
usual leadership functions—encouraging people to contribute,
keeping order, making sure the group doesn't stray off the
topic, responding to contributions, drawing out shy members
and controlling loud ones, making connections between contributions, drawing conclusions, etc.—are assumed by the
group members themselves. And if the job doesn't get done or
is done poorly, the group must also accept the consequences of
their failure to take responsibility.

Shifting from the traditional teacher-centered structure
to a group-centered structure is a difficult undertaking for
both teacher and class. Very few classes are able to undertake
activities of this type without some problems at the beginning.
Students need guidance in learning and practicing the skills
needed for success in group-centered learning activities.
Without such training, group-centered activities are likely to
be disasters. But if the teacher patiently helps students develop
the needed skills, group-centered activities can be satisfying
and successful.

Choose the right size group.

The size of a learning group should vary in accordance
with the task. For a discussion involving the expression of one's
personal opinion on a highly threatening topic, it may be wise
to limit the groups to two or three persons each. To decide an
issue which involves the entire class, such as what unit of study
to undertake next, a discussion with the whole group is needed,
even if the class has 35 or 40 students.

But tiny groups and very large groups have drawbacks:
if a group is too small, the members may not have enough
resources, expertise, and diversity of ideas to complete the task
successfully. If the group is too large, the amount of time for
each member to speak is severely limited. As a result, students
may become restless, bored, or disruptive.

Somewhere in between these two extremes lies the ideal size for most tasks. I have found that for most classroom activities five is the most effective size for a group. But when I want each student to be even more highly involved, I don't hesitate to reduce that number; and if I feel that greater diversity of opinion and skills is required, I increase the group size. I almost always conduct introductory and follow-up activities with the entire classroom group, no matter how large it is, since this is the group that constitutes the "classroom community."

Randomly assign students to small groups.

I have found the random assignment of students to groups most likely to be successful. Some authorities suggest letting students choose whom they wish to work with, but I have found that for many students this procedure is fraught with anxiety. Both choosing and being chosen are highly threatening, and I see no reason to add that burden to any others that may hinder productive group work.

Other authorities suggest that the teacher assign students to groups according to the students' personal characteristics. One such "trick" is to put all the monopolizers in a group together and let them have at one another. Another device is to group all the shy students together so that they'll be forced to talk to keep from going crazy! I feel that for the teacher to compose groupings in order to deal with problems such as monopolizing or shyness or apathy encourages students to think that problems can only be solved by the teacher's intervention, rather than encouraging students to develop the skills for working out problems themselves.

I prefer to assign students at random and then have everyone deal with whatever problems may arise. For one thing, random assignment conveys to students that all persons in the class are of equal value. When students are allowed to group themselves they generally seek out those they know or like. Random selection indicates that knowing or liking another person doesn't make that person more valuable in completing the group's task. If the Orientation Stage has been properly completed, students should feel at ease with all members of the class and don't need to seek out their special friends for security.

The simplest procedure for randomly assigning students to groups is "numbering off." Divide the number of students in the class by the number of people you want in each group. This will give the total number of groups. For example, if the group has 30 students and you want five persons in each group, you will have six groups. This is achieved by having students count off "one-two-three-four-five-six, one-two-three-four-five-six," etc., until every student has a number. Then you ask the "ones" to form a group in one part of the room, the "twos" in another, and so on.

Arrange seats in a circle.

Students should always be seated in such a way that everyone can see and hear everyone else. In most cases, this will be a circle. When students are meeting in small groups, they should pull their desks or chairs close to one another in a tight circle, with plenty of space between groups to preclude their disturbing each other.

Define explicit outcomes for tasks.

The success of a group-centered learning activity depends to a great extent on how explicit the assignment is made. In a typical teacher-centered activity, the students don't usually know the goal or outcome of the activity. The teacher has the goal in mind and takes full responsibility for leading the students there. Students just follow along, with little awareness of where they are going.

But since a group-centered activity puts leadership responsibility on the students, it is essential that they know what they are expected to accomplish. Thus, group-centered learning activities need to be "task-oriented." A good group-centered, task-oriented learning activity includes three components:

(1) the requirement that students work together as a group;

(2) a time limit for the activity;

(3) a specified end product that should result from the group effort.

A Social Studies teacher, for example, whose chosen topic was the changing nature of the U. S. presidency, might define the task somewhat as follows: "Working together as a group, come to an agreement by the end of the period on five of the most important ways in which the United States presidency has changed from the time of Grant until today." The group members could then set to work pooling their ideas, sorting through them, combining and evaluating them, and finally put together a list of five statements that the group agrees upon. They can then take responsibility for the quality of their product.

Another way of describing a group-centered activity is that it is a problem or task for the group to solve or resolve together. Ideally, the problem is one that requires the resources of more than just one group member to solve, and at the same time requires no resources that the group does not have access to.

Involve students in setting goals.

Learning activities can sometimes be successfully completed whether or not the students have any personal interest in the goal the teacher wants them to reach, particularly if extrinsic rewards (such as grades or teacher approval) are used to compensate for the lack of intrinsic interest. However, in the long run it is doubtful whether a group will continue to take active responsibility for completing assignments when group members have had no say in what they are going to do. The process of developing group responsibility must involve gradually increasing the amount of say students have in setting their learning goals.

In the early stages, you may simply wish to present several alternatives that are feasible within the confines of the required curriculum or of your own objectives for the course, and let the class choose the alternative they prefer. For example: "During the next three weeks, we will be studying poetry. We can either spend our time comparing pop song lyrics with older forms of poetry, or we can read and discuss different types of poetry on specific topics such as war, death, love. Which would you prefer?"

As students develop the ability to take on greater responsibility, you may wish to become less structured: "During the next three weeks, we will be studying poetry. Do you have any ideas about how you'd like to go about it?" Ultimately, you may wish to reduce the structure even more: "We've completed all of the requirements of the curriculum and I'd like to know how you want to spend the last three weeks of the semester. Who has a suggestion?"

Of course, there are always factors that limit the students' freedom to choose—some imposed from outside your classroom, such as district requirements, state curriculum guides, departmental budgets; others resulting from what you as the teacher would be comfortable with. But even within these limits, there is usually much more latitude for letting students participate in setting goals than most of us are willing to acknowledge. When you and your students mutually agree on what is to be learned and how it is to be learned, students can be expected to act responsibly in directing their own learning.

Serve as the group's observer and resource person—not as its leader.

After the goal has been defined for a learning activity, and groups have been formed and seated in the most effective pattern, remove yourself from the group. This signals to the students that they should not look to you for leadership. Walk around checking that all students are seated in such a way that they can participate fully in the group's work. Insist that the group remove any extra desks and fill in any empty spaces in their circles.

Note that I do not recommend that you appoint student leaders for the learning groups. Students should be allowed to decide whether they want a leader in the conventional sense; not every group wants or needs one. And if the students do decide they want one, it is they, not you, who should decide who it will be.

While students are working on the task, your role is chiefly that of an observer and resource person. But this does not mean you are not actively involved. Particularly in the early days of the Norm Establishment Stage, the class will flounder in its attempts to take responsibility for itself. Members need time to try out various new ways of behaving, and during this period you should be prepared to stand by and watch them do a less than perfect job. These are some of the most trying moments for the teacher in the entire group development process.

Janet's notations in her journal record what chaos her class went through in learning how to work together:

> *Today our class discussion was pretty bad. Actually, there was more arguing than discussion. . . . Mr. Stanford observed our discussion and I am sure that one of his criticisms will be the lack of common courtesy. It seemed like every time one person started talking, everyone else interrupted at the same time.*

The discussion sounded like a yelling session. Also, we have a hard time getting started and keeping the discussion going.

The teacher deliberately does not intervene during these floundering attempts to get organized, but at the end of the session the outcome of the group's work should be assessed honestly and weaknesses in the members' methods of working together should be examined openly. Poor results and ineffective interaction should be expected, but not excused or ignored. Problems the group encountered should be analyzed so they can be overcome next time.

In summary, the teacher's role in group-centered interaction is to make the task explicit, observe the students as they attempt to complete it (resisting the temptation to intervene to make sure they do it right) and then, when they have finished, discuss the results with them and how they might improve their functioning.

Grade the group as a whole for group-centered activities.

If you normally grade or otherwise evaluate students' performances in classroom activities, the outcome of a group-centered activity should of course also be evaluated. However, to increase group responsibility, the grade you assign should be based on your evaluation of the quality of the group product. This grade should be awarded to all members of the group, rather than grading differentially their individual contributions. This makes all members share responsibility for the group effort. More will be said about this approach to grading in the chapter on establishing the norm of cooperation.

STRUCTURED EXPERIENCES FOR ESTABLISH- ING NORM #1: GROUP RESPONSIBILITY

Since most of us are reluctant to let students flounder and fail at a content-related task, it is usually easier to give students initial practice in group-centered interaction with manufactured problems to solve, such as those in activities #1 and #3 below. These can be used in the earliest phase of the Norm Establishment Stage so that subsequent group-centered learning activities with a subject-matter focus are more successful.

The following activities are arranged in the order in which it is recommended they be utilized, since later ones build on skills and attitudes learned in earlier ones.

1. Average Age.

This exercise can be used to introduce students to group-centered interaction. It is a low-threat activity with a high possibility of success and yet it has all of the characteristics and procedures for helping students learn to organize themselves.

Arrange the class in a circle. Standing outside the circle, give the following instructions: "I am going to give you a job to do as a group to see how well and how quickly you can work together. It is a very simple task: you are to calculate the average age in years, months, and days of the members of this class (just years for younger students). You must work together as one group and the group must agree on one answer. When you have the answer, appoint one person to submit it to me." Repeat the directions until all students understand. Then step away and observe the group but do not talk to members.

After they submit their answer, check it and then lead them in a class discussion of the process they used to solve the problem. Ask questions such as: What problems did you have in getting organized? What slowed the group down? Was a leader needed? Did anyone serve as leader? How was the leader chosen? What responsibility did each group member have in solving this problem? How could the group solve the problem faster next time?

Conclude the follow-up discussion by listing on a large sheet of butcher paper or newsprint the conclusions the group comes to about working together on a group task. Save this list to post the next time you assign a group-centered learning activity. The strength of this exercise lies in the fact that it is inductive—that is, students arrive at their own principles of good group behavior as a result of experience, rather than having the teacher tell them how to organize for maximum effectiveness.

Most groups will be ready to move on to structured experience #2 after one use of experience #1, but some teachers may wish to give members a chance to put the insights gained from the first trial to work in a similar activity. You may use weight or height as the basis of the second task, or make up a new task. The key is to give students a very simple problem which every student can easily contribute to and for which there is a definite answer.

2. Forced Contribution.

Arrange the group in a circle. Standing outside the circle, assign the group a simple topic to discuss—one that every member will have some ideas about, such as "What changes should be made in our school?" Or use some content-related question that every student can be counted on to respond to, such as "What uses do Americans make of oil?"

Give the following directions: "To complete this task satisfactorily, you must meet the following requirements: Each person in the group must contribute at least once (optional: twice), and you must contribute in random order; that is, you cannot go in order around the circle. I will call time after ten minutes (adjust as necessary, depending on size of group) and by then every person must have contributed. Please begin now." To keep track of whether each person has contributed to the discussion prepare a list of the names of all the students and put a check next to each contributor's name. Or, prepare a seating diagram with each student's name in a square. Mark an X in the square each time a student contributes to the discussion.

After the specified time, talk about the activity. Begin by asking the group whether every member contributed.

Share the information in the record you kept. Then ask questions such as the following:

> Who kept order?
>
> What did you do if several persons wanted to talk at the same time?
>
> What ways were used to encourage quieter members to participate?

It might be thought that this format would increase the anxiety of students who are reluctant to contribute and thus make it even less likely that they would participate in the future. In reality, the effect is quite the opposite. Apparently, expecting all students to contribute within a time limit (and penalizing the entire group, with disapproval if not with a poor grade, if they do not) makes it easier for shyer students to take part, since they know the group needs their contribution in order to meet the requirements of the assignment.

Here's what Janet said about this activity in her personal journal:

> *Today we tried a new experiment. Within five minutes everyone in our group had to talk once, and then twice, for everyone in the group to get an "A." This time I was required to talk for everyone to get a good grade. I wasn't nervous or embarrassed to talk. The exercises that we're doing have really helped me and, I think, the rest of the class. It's made it easier for me to talk without being self-conscious. Everyone feels the same, because we're all under the same pressure.*

3. Mystery Games.

The *Mystery Games* are similar in format to the *Average Age* exercise, but instead of each student contributing a simple piece of known information, new information is distributed to the group, a different clue to each member. The process of pooling information, as in *Average Age,* is required for solving these mysteries, and thus the *Mystery Games* give students additional practice in the skills of group organization and interaction, and additional insight into the kinds of responsibilities that each member must assume if the group is to work together successfully.

General Directions for Mystery Games

The clues are different for each *Mystery Game,* but the following procedure is the same for all the games. Choose the mystery that seems most appropriate for the size, interests, and grade level of your class, or make up your own mystery, following the suggestions given later in this section.

(1) Type each clue on a slip of paper or 3″ x 5″ index card.

(2) Review with the class their list of points about working together as a group that came out of the follow-up discussion for activity #1, *Average Age.* Post the list (written on newsprint) if they made one.

(3) Arrange the class in a circle and distribute the clues so that every student has at least one. Hand out all clues, giving some students more than one if necessary. If there are not quite enough clues for every student to have at least one, give the same clue to two students. If almost half the class is without clues, divide the class into two groups, and have the two groups work on the mystery simultaneously.

(4) Give the following instructions: "Each of you has a piece of information that may or may not be useful in solving the mystery. Your task is to consider the information and arrive at the correct answer together. You may discuss the information on your cards, but you cannot pass your cards around or show them to anyone else. I will be timing you to see how quickly you solve the mystery." Add to your instructions the specific information for the mystery

you've chosen. Should you wish to grade this activity, add this information to the instructions. For example, "If you arrive at the correct solution within 10 minutes, everyone in the group will get an A; if it takes you 15 minutes, everyone gets a B; if it takes 20 minutes, a C; 25 minutes, a D, etc." (Adjust time limits to fit the maturity of the group and difficulty of the task.)

(5) Tell the group to start work; then withdraw. Start timing their work. Observe their process carefully, taking notes on what students do that is helpful and what they do that is less helpful. Let them work for at least 30 minutes. If by that time they are hopelessly confused or frustrated, call time and tell them the answer. If the group comes up with an answer before the 30 minutes are up, require them to check to see if the entire group agrees on the answer they are submitting to you. Check their answer and tell them how long it took them.

(6) Conduct a follow-up discussion focusing on how the group went about organizing for this task and how they made sure all information was shared. Use questions such as the following:

> How did you prevent everyone from talking at once?
>
> Was a formal leader needed?
>
> How did you lose time getting organized?
>
> Did you have any problems because some people didn't share their clues?
>
> Did some members ignore the clues of others?
>
> What could you have done to be sure to share all the clues?
>
> Were all members included in solving the problem?
>
> Did members make an incorrect guess because they didn't consider everyone's clues?

(7) Then ask students to compare the *Mystery Game* with an actual classroom activity. Lead them to see that group members have two important responsibilities: to contribute what they can that might be of help to the group, and to encourage other members to contribute.

(8) On a subsequent day, administer a second *Mystery Game* following the same procedure. Have students discuss how their group interaction skills have improved.

Here's how Janet reacted to this activity, as recorded in her personal journal:

> *Today one of our games was a murder mystery. It was a lot of fun. We were each given clues (two or three) about a certain incident. Our object was to discover who did it, where, when, with what, and his motive. We all worked together for once and accomplished something. The group, including me, was excited as we tried to figure out the mystery. There were a couple of leaders in the group and I wasn't one of them. I am still kind of shy in class, which surprises me. I figured that by now I'd be the "big mouth" of the class. . . .*

> *Today we solved another mystery. This time we only had to find out who did it. It took us too long to get organized, so for about 10 minutes everyone was talking at once. We ended up with a B, but just barely. I wasn't in complete agreement with the answer, but I figured that if everyone else was completely sure, I would agree, too. We weren't as well organized nor did we do as good a job as we did the first time. Why, I don't know. There were a few more kids in class this time. Also, everyone talked—but they all talked at once. At least you learn from your mistakes!*

Mystery Games For Large Groups

A. Hijacking Mystery[1] This *Mystery Game* includes 17 clues and is usually played by 17 participants. In most classes, therefore, it will be necessary to divide the class in half and have the two groups play the game concurrently. (Optional: have the two groups race to see which arrives at the correct answer first.) After distributing the clues and giving the instructions, give this explanation: "A plane was hijacked while on a flight from Hawaii to Singapore. Your job is to find out which suspect picked up by the police most likely was the hijacker."

The plane was hijacked on the evening of August 14.

The plane was ordered to fly over the island of Fani, where the hijacker parachuted from the plane in the middle of the night.

Two days after the hijacking, the Fani police rounded up five American women who fit the description of the hijacker in some way.

Annie Murkel has great interest in the religious festivals of the Fani Islanders.

Lisa Love is an archeologist who believes that man originally evolved on Fani Island and is digging for proof.

Betty Briggle is wanted in the United States for the sale of 50 pounds of marijuana.

Felicia Diamond fell in love with a Fani Islander when he was in the United States as a student.

---

[1]Printed by permission of Learning Ventures, a Multimedia Division of Bantam Books, from "Interaction" by Sweet, Blankenship, and Stanford, © 1977 by Bantam Books.

Matilda Mitchell is Betty Briggle's secretary.

The archeologist has black hair and brown eyes.

Matilda Mitchell first arrived on the island on August 16.

The police reported that a month earlier, one girl had arrived with a large, strange-looking dog in a sailboat which she had sailed from San Francisco.

When the police found Lisa Love, she was untangling a parachute from a tree.

The girl who is in love with a Fani Islander has a shepherd-collie-Samoyed mix dog named Cruiser R. Roozer.

The hijacker has light brown hair and blue eyes.

The sister of the Peace Corps worker and her secretary had arrived on the island by boat from the Philippines.

The hijacker had escaped from a mental hospital in the United States.

Betty Briggle's sister is a member of the Peace Corps who has lived on Fani Island for a year.

(The answer: Annie Murkel. All other suspects have good alibis.)

B. Kidnapping Mystery. This mystery, with 38 clues, was written by Mike Trujillo, a seventh-grader in the class of Alice Swanson at Grant Junior High School in Denver, Colorado. After you distribute the clues and announce the rules for the activity, give this explanation: "A girl named Suzy was kidnapped. Your task is to determine who kidnapped her, where he or she kept Suzy, and why she was kidnapped."

The airlines were not in operation the whole week of November 1-7.

George didn't like show business very much, but continually dreamed of getting rich.

Suzy's mother had died of cancer four years ago.

Suzy said she was knocked unconscious on the last day she was held captive and awoke in the woods just before she was found on November 4.

Because Mr. Light had spent five years in prison, he didn't have custody of his children.

Only Mr. Green knew about the playhouse.

Suzy was kidnapped sometime after school on November 1.

Mr. Green was seen sneaking around in the woods many times.

Mr. Light knew Mr. Green from his childhood.

Suzy said she was blindfolded the whole time she was kidnapped.

The only path through the woods was to Mrs. Light's house.

Bill had been unemployed since he was discharged from the army after the Vietnam war.

Mr. Light was gone November 2, 3, and 4 because of a business trip.

The ransom was paid sometime in the afternoon on November 4.

George had taught Mr. Light fancy ways of tying ropes.

The afternoon of November 1, Mrs. Light asked her gardener to transplant some chrysanthemums and noticed that he looked awfully messy.

Mr. Green had worked for Mrs. Light for 25 years and had never gotten a raise.

Mr. Light was Suzy's father.

Mr. Light owned a cabin in the mountains, which he went to often.

Mrs. Light was very rich and very stingy.

Mr. Green was Mrs. Light's gardener.

The circus left town at 3:30 p.m. on November 1 and George went with it.

Police were unable to locate Miss Smith for questioning after Suzy was kidnapped. She had apparently disappeared.

Suzy said the person who grabbed her on November 1 had dirty hands.

Mr. Light had money trouble because of a questionable financial scheme he had been involved in.

Mr. Green had built a playhouse for Suzy and her friends years ago, but later built a new one.

Bill said he saw Mr. Green come from the woods late in the afternoon on November 1.

Miss Smith returned on November 5 with Mr. Light.

Mr. Light flirted with Miss Smith, Suzy's homeroom teacher.

A ransom letter was delivered to Mrs. Light, demanding that she pay $50,000 for Suzy's release.

Suzy lived with her grandmother, Mrs. Light, in a big, old house in the woods.

November 1 was a very warm day.

Suzy had an older brother named Bill.

The police arrested Bill at 5:00 p.m. on November 1 for hitting a policeman, and he was kept in jail for 5 days and had Suzy's sweater with him.

When Suzy was walking home from school on November 1, Miss Smith offered her a ride.

Suzy was 14 years old.

George was a cowboy and rope expert in the circus.

When Suzy was found, she had rope burns on her waist and wrists, and cuts and bruises elsewhere on her body.

(Answer: Mr. Green was the kidnapper. He kept Suzy in the old playhouse until he knocked her out and left her in the woods on November 4. He had tied her to a chair and blindfolded her during the period of captivity. Mr. Green was bitter about the salary Mrs. Light paid him, and wanted more money. Miss Smith and Mr. Light couldn't have done it because they were out of town. George had left with the circus long before the ransom was paid, and Bill was in jail from the first through the fifth of November.)

Two other *Mystery Games,* a murder mystery and a bank robbery, designed for groups of approximately 30 students, can be found in *Learning Discussion Skills Through Games* by Gene Stanford and Barbara Dodds Stanford, New York: Citation Press, 1969.

Mystery Games For Small Groups[2]

To give students practice working in small groups, utilize either or both of the mysteries below, one of which has six clues and the other, five. Divide the class into small groups of five to six members each, and distribute the clues.

---

[2]Adapted from *Elements of Finite Mathematics* by A. J. Pettofrezzo. Belmont, California: Wadsworth Publishing Company, 1974. Used with permission.

C.   Who's the Cashier?   Give the following explanation: "A small business office is staffed by a manager, assistant manager, cashier, teller, clerk, and stenographer. The personnel employed are Mr. Brown, Mr. Smith, Miss Jones, Mrs. Johnson, Miss Williams, and Mr. Dean. Your task is to find out who is the cashier."

> The assistant manager is the manager's grandson.
>
> Mr. Brown is a bachelor.
>
> Mr. Smith is 21 years old.
>
> The cashier is the stenographer's son-in-law.
>
> The teller is Miss Jones' stepsister.
>
> Mr. Dean is the manager's neighbor.

(Answer: Mr. Smith.)

D.   Who's the Freshman?   Give the following explanation: "Steve, Paul, Art, Don, and Bruce are a freshman, a sophomore, a junior, a senior, and a graduate student in chemistry, engineering, medicine, law, and mathematics, but not necessarily in that order. Your task is to find out who is the freshman and who majors in engineering."

> The engineering student graduated from the same high school as Paul and Art.
>
> Bruce graduated from the law school last year with honors.
>
> Steve will become an intern next year.
>
> Paul and the sophomore mathematics student room together.
>
> Don is in a higher class than Paul.

(Answer: Paul is the freshman. Don majors in engineering.)

Subject-Matter Related Mystery Games

The *Mystery Game* format can be adapted to almost any subject matter, allowing the teacher to meet group development and subject-matter goals simultaneously. Below are three examples of *Mystery Games* especially suited for general science or health, mathematics, and chemistry. The first two games do not require any specialized knowledge other than the information provided in the game clues. The chemistry game requires a working knowledge of basic organic chemistry.

E.   The Strange Malady Mystery.   This *Mystery Game* is suitable for up to 27 participants. Based on information drawn from authentic case histories, it is especially useful for health, science, or social studies classes. After explaining the rules and distributing the clues, give the following explanation: "An epidemic has broken out on the island of Drambui. Over 300 people has been stricken with a strange disease. The World Health Organization has asked all of you to work together to try to find the cause of this epidemic. The card each of you has received indicates who you are and what information you possess. Work together as a group to decide what has caused the 300 people to become ill."

You are an investigator for the World Health Organization. You have learned that contributions to the cerebral palsy fund of Drambui doubled in 1972.

You are an investigator for the World Health Organization. You have discovered that the mercury levels in tuna fish near Drambui are very high.

You are a local physician on Drambui. You tested all 300 patients for V.D. Only Lonino had V.D.

You are a friend of Jomo's family. You know that his daughter fell on her head when she was a few months old.

You are a Drambuian named Jomo. Your seven-year-old daughter is blind and unable to walk or talk. You began to notice her symptoms in April, 1972.

You are an investigator for the World Health Organization. You have discovered that a British paper mill was started in Drambui in October, 1972, and uses mercury in its process. The mill dumps wastes into the water.

You are a Drambui Islander named Rev. Kova. You know that sexual activity among the young people of Drambui has been rapidly increasing and a lot of American tourists have recently come to your island. You suspect that the incidence of V.D. is increasing.

You are a Drambui Islander who knows that Drambui Islanders consider tuna sacred and don't eat it.

You are a friend of Moni. You know that Moni worked during 1971 in the United States in an atomic energy plant. An accident occurred when he was there that released some radiation.

You are a Drambuian named Moni. You began suffering from severe nausea in March of 1972. Next, you had diarrhea attacks and your skin turned lead-colored.

You are a Drambuian named Lina. You had a baby in November, 1972, who was born blind and retarded and does not seem to be developing normally in other physical respects.

You are a member of the World Health Organization who has discovered that the United States tested two H-bombs in 1969 about 200 miles from Drambui.

You are a member of the World Health Organization investigating team. You have learned that the islanders imported wheat seed from Sweden in 1971 and 1972.

You are a member of the World Health Organization

investigating team. You have found through research that in Sweden, the U.S.A., and several other countries, wheat seed is treated with mercury to reduce spoiling.

You are a medical specialist with the World Health Organization. You know that symptoms of atomic radiation sickness include nausea, faintness, diarrhea, and sometimes the skin turns a leaden color.

You are a medical specialist on the World Health Organization team. You know that symptoms of syphilis can include blindness, incoherent speech, and paralysis.

You are a World Health Organization specialist in farming. You have discovered that some farmers feed wheat seed to their pigs instead of planting it.

You are a medical specialist with the World Health Organization. You know that cerebral palsy is caused by damage to the brain before or during birth.

You are the oldest living Drambuian. You remember an ancient legend which stated that a strange white-skinned people would bring horrible diseases to your island. You maintain that the only hope for the Drambuians is to get rid of all foreigners.

You are a Drambui Islander named Koreko. In April, 1972, you became completely blind and are now having difficulty speaking and walking.

You are a medical specialist for the World Health Organization. You know that symptoms of mercury poisoning include convulsions, problems in walking, visual problems, including blindness, and difficulty in speaking.

You are a medical specialist with the World Health Organization. You know that mercury has been used as a treatment for syphilis.

You are a Drambui Islander named Lonino. You

know that in January, 1972, you developed convulsions, and became unable to speak clearly, walk steadily, or write steadily.

You are a Drambuian who knows that ham is a favorite food of all the islanders.

You are a Drambui Islander named Roga. Starting in June, 1972, you began to have dizzy spells, headaches, and tremors. In October you began to have trouble speaking clearly.

You are a member of the World Health Organization who knows that symptoms of cerebral palsy are muscular incoordination and speech disturbances.

You are a Drambui Islander and a friend of Lonino. You know that Lonino is a vegetarian and does not eat any kind of meat or fish.

(Answer: The epidemic was caused by mercury poisoning produced by contaminated wheat seed fed to pigs.)

F.   Math Mystery.   This mystery is designed for 13 participants; classes should be divided into groups to work on the game simultaneously. After distributing the clues, announce: "A man drove from Waterville, through Adamston and Scott City, to Beaverberg. Your task is to calculate how long it took him to make this trip. The problem is complicated by the fact that strange new units of time and distance are used. You'll have to use these new terms in order to solve the problem. The problem is: how many 'wors' did it take the man to drive from Waterville to Beaverberg?"

It is 4 lutts from Waterville to Adamston.

It is 8 lutts from Adamston to Scott City.

It is 10 lutts from Scott City to Beaverberg.

A lutt is 10 mipps.

A mipp is a way of measuring distance.

There are 2 mipps in a mile.

A dar is 10 wors.

A wor is 5 mirs.

A mir is a way of measuring time.

There are two mirs in an hour.

The man drives from Waterville to Adamston at the rate of 24 lutts per wor.

The man drives from Adamston to Scott City at a rate of 30 lutts per wor.

The man drives from Scott City to Beaverberg at the rate of 30 lutts per wor.

(Answer: 23/30 wors)

G. Molecular Model Mystery. The following activity was devised by John Brady, a chemistry teacher at New Hartford (New York) High School. Divide the class into small groups. In this game, each group has a different problem to solve. Distribute a set of clues to each group and instruct each student to take a clue. Announce: "Each of you has a card that contains one piece of information which, when pooled with information held by other members of your group, identifies a specific compound. Decide as a group the name of the compound (using IUPAC nomenclature) and draw the structural formula for it. When your group has arrived at an answer, tell me and I'll check it. Then you can exchange your set of clues with other groups to identify other compounds."

Compound #1:

This molecule is a saturated hydrocarbon.

This compound contains two alkyl groups.

The alkyl groups are bonded to different carbon atoms.

The longest chain contains five carbon atoms.

This compound is an isomer of octane.

(Answer: 2-methyl-3-ethylpentane)

Compound #2:

This molecule contains eleven carbon atoms.

One alkyl group is on the fourth carbon atom.

This molecule contains four alkyl groups.

Two alkyl groups are on the second carbon atom.

The longest chain contains seven carbon atoms.

One alkyl group is on the third carbon atom.

This molecule is a saturated hydrocarbon.

(Answer: 2,2,3,4-tetramethylheptane)

Compound #3:

A chlorine atom is on each end of the chain.

This molecule contains four halogen atoms.

This molecule contains one triple bond.

This molecule contains four carbon atoms.

A bromine atom is on each end of the chain.

(Answer: 1,4-dibromo-4, 4-dichloro 2-butyne)

Compound #4:

This molecule contains one alkyl group.

The longest chain contains four carbon atoms.

This molecule is a secondary alcohol.

This molecule contains five carbon atoms.

(Answer: 3-methyl-2-butanol)

Compound #5:

One of the reactants is a common primary alcohol containing two carbon atoms.

One of the products is water.

This molecule is made from an esterification reaction.

The second reactant is a common organic acid containing two carbon atoms.

(Answer: ethyl acetate)

Compound #6:

This molecule contains two alkyl groups.

Both alkyl groups are attached to the same carbon atom.

The longest chain contains seven carbon atoms.

This molecule fits the general formula C_nH_{2n+2}.

This molecule contains 13 carbon atoms.

(Answer: 4,4-dipropylheptane.)

Writing Your Own Mystery Games

To write your own *Mystery Game* to fit the subject-matter goals of a unit you are teaching, choose a topic in which a general conclusion can be drawn from a large number of separate pieces of information. In social studies, for example, a *Mystery Game* could be used to explore the relationship between culture and climate. Each member could be given a description of an artifact found at an archeological site or in an existing town, and the group could be asked to decide which of several locations (a mountainous location, a seacoast, or a forest) was probably the site of the village. For a vocabulary *Mystery Game* in English, each student in a small group could be given a sentence containing the same unfamiliar word and the group could be asked to determine the meaning of the new word.

After choosing the specific subject matter for your game, divide the information into small pieces and give each student one bit of information. Provide all the facts the group needs to solve the mystery, rather than assuming that students will fill in with what they remember from previous reading and class discussion. Be sure there are no individual clues which give away the answer. The game is more challenging and beneficial if a large number of pieces of information must be combined to arrive at the answer. You might also add some "distractors," pieces of irrelevant or misleading information. But be sure that there are clues that will explain or counter-act the distractors.

For the first few subject-matter *Mystery Games*, it is best to have the solution be an answer that can be judged correct—i.e., there should be a right or wrong answer. However, it is possible to utilize the *Mystery Game* format to have the group make a judgment instead of reaching a factual conclusion. For example, you could give each student one piece of information supporting the guilt or innocence of a defendant in a trial and have the class decide whether the accused should be convicted. Or you could give as clues findings from research studies about the effects of a new drug and ask the class to decide whether the Food and Drug Administration should allow it to be produced and sold.

A further variation for subject-matter oriented *Mystery Games* could require each student to write a clue for a specific topic by doing research. For example, the task of the group could be to determine what level of civilization Africa had reached before the coming of the Europeans, and each student could be assigned to research a specific African society. Each student would contribute research findings to a total class discussion, and the group members would come to an agreement on how civilized Africa was.

In general, it is best to move a group from the tightly structured, non-subject-matter oriented mysteries to a subject-matter mystery in which exact clues are provided, and finally have them work on a subject-matter mystery for which they must obtain their own information to contribute.

4. Drawing Out A Speaker.

As a result of their experiences with the previous activities, students will have become aware that for group-centered interaction to succeed they themselves must assume responsibility for a number of things that have traditionally been the *teacher's* responsibility. One of these is the responsibility for getting all members of the group to contribute. Since students are likely to have had little opportunity to learn how to encourage others to contribute, some deliberate training in this skill is usually necessary.

Ask students to help you make a list on the board of ways one person can help draw out another person; that is, how one person can encourage another to talk and continue talking. The list might include:

> Looking directly at the speaker
>
> Nodding to show you are listening
>
> "Sitting it out" during pauses rather than rushing to respond
>
> Asking questions that cause the speaker to explain in more detail

Discuss with the class how these behaviors differ from the way listeners in a group normally act. Explore the effects of arguing and disagreeing on a discussion.

Then divide the class into pairs and have the partners sit facing each other. Give the following instructions: "One of you is to be the Speaker and the other is to be the Encourager. The Speaker is to give a detailed answer to the question, 'What personal qualities do you value most in a friend?' The Encourager is to use the ideas we listed on the board to respond in a way that draws the Speaker out. I will call time after five minutes. Encouragers, see if you can keep your Speakers talking for the entire time."

After five minutes call time and have the partners discuss questions such as the following:

> If you were the Speaker, did you feel the Encourager was genuinely interested in hearing what you had to say?
>
> What did the Encourager do that made you want to continue talking?
>
> What did the Encourager do that discouraged you from talking more?
>
> Did the Encourager argue or disagree?
>
> Did the Encourager ever start talking about herself or himself?
>
> If you were the Encourager, what problems did you have in keeping the Speaker talking?
>
> Were you ever tempted to "take over" the conversation, focusing on yourself rather than on the Speaker?
>
> What techniques seemed to be useful in encouraging the Speaker to keep talking?

Then have the partners change roles and repeat the activity.

5. Drawing Out in Group Discussion.

Divide a large class into two or more smaller groups, with each group seated in a circle. Review the ways of encouraging another person to talk. Point out that these same techniques can be used in a group discussion to encourage all members to contribute fully.

Assign the group a topic to discuss which is somewhat personal, so that every student will have ideas about it, and at the same time a bit controversial. For example, "What is the most important thing for a person to learn in school?"

Instruct the group about how they can put into practice in their discussion the procedures for drawing out a speaker. Suggest that whenever a member has something to contribute to the discussion that person be considered the Speaker (as in *Drawing Out a Speaker,* above) and all other members of the group act as Encouragers, helping to draw out the Speaker until that person has said everything he or she wants to. The same procedure is followed each time someone wishes to contribute to the discussion.

As the discussion proceeds, monitor the interaction of the students carefully. You may need to stop them from time to time to point out instances where students did not act as Encouragers while someone was talking. After about 15 minutes, call time and discuss what happened:

Why is it hard to play the Encourager role in a group discussion?

What's the advantage of drawing out people in a group discussion rather than arguing or rushing to contribute your own ideas?

What techniques seem to be helpful in encouraging everyone to contribute ideas to a group discussion?

6. Rhythm Transformations.

This activity allows the group to explore the concepts of emerging leadership and changing leadership as they are reflected in a nonverbal activity. Arrange the class in a circle, seated or standing. Have one student start clapping in a simple basic rhythm and instruct the rest of the class to follow this student, clapping in the same rhythm. Then tell the class that you would like someone—anyone—in the group to change the rhythm, but to do this without saying anything. The person is just to start a new rhythm and the rest of the class is to follow the new rhythm. Tell the group to stay with one rhythm until it is well established—that is, until everyone is together; then whoever wants to can initiate a new rhythm.

After five or six changes have been made, stop and discuss the activity: "How did the group know when someone wanted to lead the class into a new rhythm? Were there times when the group chose not to follow a new rhythm that was introduced? What caused you to introduce—or kept you from introducing—a new rhythm? Why is it hard to take the lead in an activity like this?" (Variations: add body movements or abstract vocal sounds to the clapping.)

7. New Roles.

Based on their experience with group-centered exercises, have the class help you draw' up a list on a piece of newsprint or butcher paper of all the ways that a good group member can take responsibility for the group to achieve its goal. Remind the students about the things you observed various group members do that were helpful. After students have brainstormed helpful membership behavior, combine and summarize their contributions into four categories, as follows:

> *Organizing*—starting things moving, suggesting a plan of action, keeping the group on the topic, reminding the group of their goal, calling for a vote
>
> *Contributing*—sharing whatever information or ideas or other resources one has
>
> *Encouraging*—calling on other members to contribute, listening in *such* a way that draws out other members
>
> *Making Connections*—linking contributions together, pointing out the relationship between ideas, summarizing.

You might wish to point out that in the typical teacher-led learning activity the teacher usually performs all these functions (except for contributing). To further clarify what behavior is involved in each of these roles, ask for examples of the sort of thing a person playing that role might say; for example, what might a person taking responsibility for organizing the group say to the group?

Then, to give the class additional practice with these four types of group membership behaviors, arrange the class in a circle and hand each student a card on which you have written one of the group member responsibilities. (For best results, distribute only two or three "Organizing" cards.) Tell students not to let anyone else see what responsibility they were assigned. Announce a topic for the group to discuss, either a subject-matter question or a controversial issue, such as "Should the U.S. have spent the billions of dollars that it took to send a man to the moon?" Instruct students that during the discussion they are to play the roles they were assigned and that at the end of the discussion everyone will try to guess what role each person was assigned. Emphasize that although in most discussions participants choose which responsibility they will assume, changing from one to another when appropriate, for the purpose of this activity students should stick to the one assigned role as much as possible.

After about 10 or 15 minutes, call time and let the members guess what role each person was playing. If any members had trouble playing their roles, ask them to explain why and have other members suggest how they could have improved. Point out again that in most classroom activities members can play any of the roles they choose and it is not necessary to restrict oneself to a single role.

8. Choose a Mascot.

This activity gives students additional practice in assuming the responsibilities of effective group members and helps them explore further how leadership emerges in a group that doesn't have an assigned leader. Prepare sets of from eight to ten cards assigning the following roles to group members:

CARD NUMBER	INFORMATION ON CARD
1	Role you are to play: Organizing
2	Role you are to play: Any you wish or none at all. You have the special knowledge that the group is going to be asked to select a chairperson later in the exercise. You are to conduct yourself in such a manner that the members will select you as chair person. But don't let them know you have advance knowledge of the up-coming election!
3	Role you are to play: Contributing
4	Role you are to play: Any you wish or none at all. You have the special knowledge that the group is going to be asked to select a chairperson later in the

	exercise. You are to conduct yourself in such a manner that the members will select you as chairperson. But don't let them know you have advance knowledge of the up-coming election!
5	Role you are to play: Contributing
6	Role you are to play: Making Connections
7	Role you are to play: Encouraging Others
8	Role you are to play: Encouraging Others
9	Role you are to play: Contributing
10	Role you are to play: Making Connections

Divide the class into small groups of 8-10 persons and have them arrange their desks into tight circles. (Variation: have the class work as a total group seated in one large circle, and prepare enough cards so that each student has one.) Give the following explanation: "Your task as a group is to choose a mascot for your group. You will have 15 minutes in which to complete this task. I will be giving each of you a card which will assign you a role to play in your group during the discussion of what mascot to choose. Try to stick to your assigned role so that the group can later guess what role you were playing. Do not show anyone the card I give you." Distribute the cards and watch carefully that students do not reveal the contents to others. After 15 minutes, call time and ask each group to report what they chose for a mascot.

Then give these instructions: "Continue to keep the roles assigned on your card a secret. Take five or ten minutes to elect a chairperson for your group." After students have selected a chairperson, conduct a discussion focusing on the following questions:

> Can you guess what role each person in your group played?
> Could each person have done anything to play the role more effectively?
> Is there some way in which the effectiveness of your work as a group could have been improved?
> How did you elect the chairperson for your group?
> What did the persons with advance knowledge do to try to get themselves elected?
> Was their behavior effective? Did you choose one of them for your chairperson? Why or why not?
> What have you learned about how a group leader is recognized and chosen? How should a person who wants to be a leader act?

After the discussion, you may wish to have the chairpersons meet at the front of the classroom and, as representatives of their groups, decide on a mascot for the entire class.

9. Practicing Roles.

Arrange the class in a circle (or divide into several small groups). Assign students a topic to discuss—either a subject-matter task or a controversial issue, such as "What are the three best things and three worst things that have taken place in this class so far this year?"

Instruct students to deliberately attempt to play any or all of the four group membership roles (organizing, contributing, encouraging, making connections). Emphasize that they do not have to stick to a single role throughout the discussion.

Before the discussion starts, choose one or two students from each group to serve as observers. Provide the observers with forms such as the one below. Instruct them to fill in the names of the persons in the group and to note every time a person plays one of the roles during the discussion.

After the discussion, have the observers share the data they have collected. Use it as the basis of further discussion of the group's performance and effectiveness.

	MEMBERSHIP ROLE			
Name of Group Member	Organizing Discussion	Contributing Ideas	Encouraging Others	Making Connections

OBSERVER'S FORM

10. Specialized Roles.

For some classroom activites involving small groups or work teams it is helpful if particular responsibilities are assumed by each member of the team. For example, if a group is planning and executing a Thanksgiving bulletin board, one person could have the task of keeping a record of the group's decisions, another might secure all equipment and materials the group needs, and another could observe the group's functioning and point out how members can improve, etc. To utilize this approach, help the group write a description for each role needed and then let the members of the group decide which person will take each role.

Making the transition from having the teacher assume the responsibility for most classroom activites to having students assume the responsibility themselves is a very difficult process. Learning how to play their new roles requires much practice and experience for both teacher and students. The activities described in this chapter are designed to promote the new skills. The teacher and the students will themselves improvise activities of their own. The important thing is that the skills acquired in the practice activities be applied in the everyday life of the class.

4 STAGE TWO: ESTABLISHING NORMS GOAL TWO: RESPONDING TO OTHERS

It is not easy to undo what years of schooling have created. Students cling tenaciously to the patterns of interaction they have been conditioned to follow. After years of listening and responding only to the teacher, it takes time and encouragement for them to break away and feel comfortable with student-to-student interaction. Helping students get to know one another better (in the Orientation Stage) is a useful first step in fostering student-to-student interaction. And the activities that promoted norm #1, Group Responsibility, helped too. But if a group is to become truly mature and productive, deliberate attention must be given to changing the students' interaction patterns from exchanges between teacher and student to exchanges among students. This involves improving both the students' listening habits and the ways in which they contribute to class activities.

Students are rarely, if ever, taught the important social skill of being a good listener. Most students use the time when other students are talking as a chance to daydream, if they aren't interested in what's happening, or to rehearse a reply, if

117

they are. Consequently, they either never really hear one another, or they respond to what they *think* the other person meant.

Nor are students ever taught the skill of responding to one another. Analyze almost any class discussion and you'll observe what I've come to call the "skyrocket" phenomenon. When a person contributes it's equivalent to shooting up a skyrocket. The others in the group may look at it, may "ooh" and "ah" over it, but when the student is finished, all they do is wait for the next member to shoot off a different skyrocket— that is, introduce a new and more spectacular idea to the discussion, even if it is unrelated to what has gone before. The contributors may feel pleased that they have made important additions to the discussion, but even if participation is wide-spread the discussion rarely leads anywhere. New ideas are, of course, essential for a good discussion, and providing additional information is an important function for a group member. But unless connections are made between the ideas presented, unless the pieces are put together into a group product, the discussion is rarely effective.

Sometimes, certainly, the purpose of a discussion may only be to share one's experiences or opinions, with no particular goal beyond hearing what everyone has to say about the topic. This is sometimes called *open-ended* discussion, because it leads nowhere specific. However, most learning activities require the group to arrive at a decision, an answer, or the solution to a problem. And in order to do so members must link their contributions rather than just adding unrelated ideas to the heap for others to hear and then ignore.

Actually, in order to interrelate ideas, students have to listen carefully to other members to see how or whether their ideas fit and the extent to which they agree or disagree with previous speakers. Then when they enter the discussion they can indicate the relationships between their ideas and the contributions of others. To teach students good listening and responding habits is not simple. It requires changes in the teacher's behavior, as well as activities that train students in the needed skills.

HELPFUL TEACHER BEHAVIOR FOR ESTABLISHING NORM #2: RESPONDING TO OTHERS

You can influence to a great extent the way students listen and respond to one another by the way you interact verbally with your students and by the way you structure your classroom activities.

Arrange seating so that students can hear and see one another.

It is virtually impossible to have productive student-to-student interaction when all most students can see are the backs of the heads of the persons sitting in front of them. An arrangement in which all students are facing the teacher, with their backs to other students, conveys the message, "It's important to talk only to the teacher." An arrangement such as a circle or a horseshoe in which all students face each other conveys a different message: "It's important to talk to one another." To reinforce this message the teacher may sit in a student's desk as part of the circle, or may move outside the circle entirely.

Redirect questions instead of answering them yourself.

Imagine, for example, that during a discussion in your American history class Charlie asks you, "How could the early settlers of this country be so cruel and stupid as to drive the Indians off the land that really belonged to them? Wasn't that just like invading another country?" Your impulse is to answer the question posed by Charlie, supporting the action of the settlers, or agreeing with Charlie that it was deplorable, or taking some position in between. However, if you wish to foster student-to-student interaction, you can simply reply, "Yes, that's an important question, Charlie. Who has some ideas about the question Charlie is raising?" Thus you have praised Charlie for asking the question, but have indicated to the other students that you expect them to answer Charlie, rather than keeping the focus on yourself.

Albert E. Roark, in the Leader's Guide for *Becoming: A Course in Human Relations*,[1] provides an excellent explanation of the use of redirecting in a classroom discussion:

> Need for redirecting occurs frequently in the early stages of groups before group members have become skillful in conducting discussions. . . . Skillful redirecting early in group discussions helps insure wide participation and helps keep the group on appropriate subjects.
>
> Because groups in early stages of development tend to address their remarks to the leader more often than desirable, the leader's first use of redirecting is frequently to redirect a remark to someone other than himself. Jane (to leader): 'Mr. Bumgartner, why do we have to sit in a circle all the time?' Mr. Bumgartner (redirecting): 'Well, does anybody have any ideas?' This is redirecting to the group as a whole and generally has different implications than redirecting to a particular person. There are several points to be noted in Mr. Bumgartner's response: 1) he did not answer the question, 2) he treated the question to him as an important question even though he did not answer it, 3) he did not ask for an answer that implied

---

[1]Chester R. Cromwell, William Ohs, Albert E. Roark, and Gene Stanford, *Becoming: A Course in Human Relations*, Philadelphia, Pa.: J. B. Lippincott, 1975. Used with permission of the publisher.

that he was right about sitting in circles (e.g., he did not say, 'Who wants to tell Jane why it's a good idea to sit in a circle?') but instead left it open for any kind of comment, and 4) no particular person was put on the spot to come up with an answer.

Use redirection when students aren't listening to one another.

Redirecting can be used to compel students to listen closely to one another. Let's look at this exchange in a health class:

Jeff: "If putting fluoride in drinking water has been proven to help prevent tooth decay, how come our town hasn't done it?"

Teacher: "That's a good question. Would you have any ideas on that, Kim?"

Kim: "Huh? I didn't hear what he said."

Teacher: "Jeff asked why our town doesn't fluoridate the water."

In this example, the teacher repeated Jeff's question to prevent Kim from being embarrassed. Assuming that the teacher had a reason for calling on Kim particularly (because his attention had wandered) instead of redirecting Jeff's question to the class as a whole, a better response from the teacher would have been:

Teacher: "Then ask Jeff to repeat his question."

Kim: "Jeff, what did you say?"

Jeff: "I asked why our town doesn't fluoridate the water."

Kim: "Oh, well, I guess it's because the Citizens' Council campaigned so hard against it

> before the referendum. Remember, they said the Communists could use the fluoridation system to poison us and take over the country."

By requiring Kim to ask Jeff to repeat his question, the teacher has redirected the focus of interaction to the students. If the teacher continues to redirect statements such as Kim's "I didn't hear what he said," very soon all members of the class will catch on that in this class it is necessary for students to listen closely to one another because the teacher is not going to play "switchboard" for communications between students.

Do not echo every contribution.

A habit many teachers lapse into which perpetuates students' not listening to one another is restating students' answers to the teacher's questions. Here's how a typical teacher-led discussion often sounds:

Teacher: "How would you decide whether a doctor you want to go to is qualified? (hands go up) Jimmy?"

Jimmy: "I'd ask what medical school the doctor graduated from. My brother's interested in going to med school and he told me what the best ones are."

Teacher: "Okay, Jimmy would base his decision on where the doctor got his or her training. How about someone else? Laurie?"

Laurie: "I'd call up the County Medical Society and ask them if the doctor is any good."

Teacher: "Laurie would ask the County Medical Society. What else could you do? Michael?"

Michael: "I'd ask other doctors what they thought of this doctor."

Teacher: "Michael says he'd ask other doctors. What would you do, Andy?"

Andy: "I'd ask how many patients the doctor has. If it's a lot, I'd know my choice must be good."

Teacher: "Andy thinks the size of the doctor's practice is a good indicator. Do you agree, class?"

As strange as it may seem when we see it on paper, the pattern of questioning reproduced above occurs continuously in most classrooms. This habit of repeating reinforces students in the habit of not listening. Why bother, when the teacher is going to repeat everything anyway? It communicates to the students that they don't need to listen to one another, only to the teacher. When the teacher refrains from repeating and, if students haven't heard, redirects them to ask the speaker to repeat, students begin to listen to each other more attentively.

Do not allow nonlisteners to make new contributions.

If during a classroom discussion it is apparent that certain students who are making new contributions have not been listening carefully to previous speakers, do not allow them to share their own ideas until they have established that they know specifically what the preceding contributors were saying. Often a new contribution is obviously an interruption. The student has not been listening but has just been waiting for a chance to shoot up a personal skyrocket. Such a contribution generally steers the discussion in an inappropriate direction, or leaves the previous issue unresolved. Sometimes the contributor of a new idea has obviously misunderstood the previous contribution. It's often obvious when a student who wants to contribute to a discussion has been inattentive and thus is not in tune with the direction the discussion has been taking.

In all these cases, you should not allow such students to make a new contribution until they can demonstrate a knowledge of what's been said before. If students have been inattentive or have misunderstood previous contributions, it's helpful to require them to summarize what has already been said to the satisfaction of those members who made the previous contributions. This helps establish the norm that students must listen carefully to others before they can contribute their own ideas.

Reward only the behavior you want.

You should monitor closely the kinds of student behavior you reward. For example, it's easy to fall into the trap of praising a student who has contributed a brilliant new idea to the discussion—a spectacular skyrocket—even though that student fails to demonstrate how the new idea fits into the discussion. Such praise rewards the student for shooting skyrockets rather than building a group product. A better response would be to acknowledge that the idea is a good one (to reinforce the student for participating), but to point out that the student has not linked it to the rest of the discussion and ask the student to do so.

You can use praise to encourage the kinds of linking and responding behavior that are helpful in a discussion. When students show the connection between their own new idea and previous contributions, or point out how two or more ideas are related, the students should be praised deliberately and profusely by the teacher: "Sonya, I'm pleased with the way you linked Penny's and Mark's suggestions; they're really very similar and you helped us to see those similarities. Very good!" There are few influences on students' classroom behavior more powerful than the approval of the teacher. When the teacher praises a specific act by a student, the student usually gets a warm glow inside and attempts to repeat that behavior as often as possible. Therefore, every time you notice a student behaving in a helpful way during a discussion, deliberately point out that you are pleased with it.

Model the behavior you want students to display.

Students tend to imitate the teacher's behavior, even though they may not be conscious of it or willing to admit it. If the teacher does not utilize good listening habits, students are not likely to. Some basic principles of good listening are described below. If applied in your everyday interaction in the classroom, they can set an example that students may follow in interacting with each other.

Principles of Good Listening

Focus on the speaker.   The person who is speaking should be the *focus* of the conversation. Imagine that the speaker is on stage with the spotlight on him or her. This is the speaker's show. Your job is to listen, not talk. As long as the speaker is "on stage," the speaker is the focus of the conversation, and you are a facilitator; your job is to assist this person in communicating his or her ideas and feelings to you. Therefore, you should never do anything that draws the focus to yourself, that puts you in the spotlight. Your responses, while you are the listener or facilitator, should all be aimed at encouraging the speaker.

This concept of the speaker as focus of a conversation is contrary to what most of us have done habitually over the years. In the conventional notions of conversation and discussion, the object is to talk, not particularly to listen. Often the analogy of throwing a ball back and forth is used. One person talks for a few minutes, then stops and tosses the ball to another person, who begins to talk for a while. Rarely is a person listening very closely to another, because in this type of interaction the premium is placed on what you say, not on how you listen.

If you deliberately choose to play an active listening role, that is, if you choose to facilitate the other person's talking, you will not steal the spotlight for yourself. For example, if a student speaks up and says, "I don't think you're a fair grader," you might have the impulse to explain, to try to convince the student. But this means taking the focus off the student and putting it on yourself. A far more helpful response would be, "Can you tell me why you feel that way?" This response encourages students to continue talking, exploring their own thoughts and feelings, rather than making students listen to the teacher's explanation.

Look at the speaker and signal you are listening.   To help keep the focus on the speaker, look directly at the person who is talking. Look straight into the speaker's eyes. This will show the speaker that you are paying full attention and care about what is being said. Nod your head frequently as a signal that you're receiving the message and utter "uh-huh" or "umm-hummm" from time to time. It's amazing how eye contact and a nodding head can encourage a speaker, and how fast averted eyes or a turned head can turn the speaker off. Active listening, then, requires both looking at the speaker and showing that you're receiving the message.

Some people mistakenly think that nodding their heads when listening implies that they are agreeing with everything the speaker is saying. A nod or "uh-huh" means simply "I'm hearing you," nothing more. In fact, in good listening, you do not wish to signal agreement or disagreement until after the speaker is completely finished. We all have the impulse to indicate to the other person immediately what *we* think. We begin agreeing (or, more frequently, disagreeing) as soon as the words are out of the speaker's mouth. Or we begin immediately to give suggestions and advice. But the speaker's primary need is to know that you are hearing and understanding what is being said—not to have you agree, disagree, judge, give advice, or make suggestions. There may be a place for all of these later, but at first it's best to simply signal that you're listening.

Don't be afraid of silence.

Active listening requires keeping your mouth shut much of the time. When the speaker pauses, resist the impulse to fill the silence with chatter. Chances are the speaker will continue talking when it's apparent that you're willing to continue listening. If the pause lasts so long that it becomes uncomfortable, ask a question that will encourage the speaker to talk some more. Use an open-ended question—that is, one which does not have a yes/no answer or which cannot be answered with only a few words. For example, after a student has raised an issue or expressed a reaction about something, ask, "Can you tell me more about that?" or say, "I'd like to hear more about what you're feeling."

React to the speaker's comments.

In addition to feeling compelled to explain or disagree, often teachers simply do not react at all to what a student is saying. I've watched a number of teachers, particularly student teachers or beginning teachers, asking their students a series of questions about a reading assignment. The teacher will pose a question and call on a student to answer. But while the student is answering it is apparent that the teacher is busy thinking up (or searching through notes for) the next question and isn't paying attention to what the student is saying. As soon as the student finishes speaking, if the answer sounded even halfway suitable, the teacher replies with, "Fine, Terry. Now who knows why the Nile valley was such good farming land?" and calls on another student to answer the new question. The teacher does not react to the content of the first student's answer, does not *respond* to the student, but merely proceeds down a grocery list of questions.

The teacher who *attends* closely to the students' answers encourages students to expand on their answer, encourages other students to react to the answer and elaborate on it, and builds on the answer before moving on to the next question. One of the best ways I've found to break myself of poor listening habits while teaching a class was deliberately not to plan what to ask in a class discussion, relying instead on what emerged from the students. Rather than bringing into class a list of preplanned questions, I'd start with one basic, open-ended question such as "What thoughts do you have about the assignment you had for today?" or "How do you feel about the way . . . ?" This forced me to listen closely to what students were saying and to respond meaningfully rather than rushing on to another question. I am not recommending that teachers not plan lessons carefully, but I am suggesting that trying this approach for a couple of days is a way to improve one's own listening habits.

Restate or summarize what you've heard.   I have indicated earlier that repeating students' answers can have the harmful result of encouraging students not to listen to one another. This is particularly true when students are giving short, factual answers to a series of questions. However, there are occasions when restating or summarizing what a speaker has said can be a valuable part of active listening. These are the occasions when a student has described in some detail ideas or feelings of personal significance. For example, when a student complains about something you've done, or shares some personal views on a controversial or somewhat threatening topic, restating or summarizing what the student has said shows that you've understood and encourages the student to continue speaking.

When it is clear that the speaker has finished one aspect of the discussion, you may paraphrase the main idea expressed, showing that you have understood and giving the speaker the opportunity to explain more fully if there is something you have misunderstood. For an illustration, let's go back to the student who complained about your grading procedures:

Jerry: "I don't think you're a fair grader.

Ms. Lynch: (*drawing out*) "Can you tell me more about why you feel that way?"

Jerry: "Yeah, you didn't give me any credit for using the right method. Just because I got the answer wrong you marked the whole problem wrong. And you did it five times!"

Ms. Lynch: (*restating*) "You feel I should have given you some credit for knowing how to work the problem, even if you made careless errors and got the wrong answers."

Jerry: "Yeah, the important thing is knowing how to work the problem, and I obviously showed I could do that. As it turned out, I got the same low grade as four or five people in here who didn't even attempt to work the problems 'cause they didn't know how."

Ms. Lynch: (*restating*) "You feel you deserve a higher grade."

Jerry: "I sure do! It's one thing not to know how to work the problems and another to just make careless errors."

Ms. Lynch: (*restating*) "You'd like me to change the grading procedure to differentiate between not knowing at all and making careless errors."

Notice that Ms. Lynch resisted the impulse to explain why she considers careless errors just as serious as not knowing how to work the problem. We assume that ultimately she may get to that. But initially she devotes her attention to showing Jerry that she understands what he's telling her, and she does this by summarizing (or restating, or paraphrasing) what she hears. This lets Jerry know that she really cares about what he has to say, that she isn't going to condemn him for objecting to the way she graded, and that she is seriously trying to understand his objections. She is not necessarily agreeing with what he's saying, but neither is she rushing to point out that he is wrong. Note especially that the teacher's responses are phrased as declarative sentences, not questions. For example, stating "You feel you deserve a higher grade," conveys understanding, whereas asking "You feel you deserve a higher grade?" can become a signal of rejection and disagreement, as if you were saying, "Do you really have the audacity to think that you deserve a better grade than the one I gave you?!"

Respond to feeling messages.   The feelings conveyed in an exchange in the classroom are frequently as important as the verbal message itself. For example, Jerry, in the example above, is indicating all sorts of things about his feelings, such as "I'm mad at you for giving me a low grade," "I feel bad that my grade is so low even though I knew how to work the problems," "I'm embarrassed that I made careless errors." He does not say these things directly (few of us do talk about our feelings openly), but the teacher who is listening well will perceive the feelings beneath the cognitive message and will respond to these as well as to the words.

To understand the feelings conveyed in a message, ask yourself, "How is this person feeling? Is the student angry, hurt, afraid, pleased, proud, smug, uncertain, annoyed, embarrassed, nervous, enthusiastic?" Often, non-verbal clues will help you perceive the speaker's feelings. Look at the student's posture and gestures, listen to the tone of voice. Ask yourself, "How would I feel if I were saying that?"

When you think you perceive the feelings, respond to them. Usually this can be done with a simple statement, such as "You seem angry with me because of the grade I gave you." The tone of voice you use in making such a statement is extremely important. You should try to convey understanding and sympathy. Be careful not to sound surprised by the feelings, or disapproving of them. Use a gentle tone of voice, one that expresses caring rather than judging.

Make linking statements in discussions. In class discussions, where a number of students are involved, you can model good responding behavior by deliberately making linking statements. For example, "Both of you seem to support the Israeli position; but Thad, you seem to be more convinced than Wendy that we should provide military aid. Is that right?" Or you may summarize what the discussion has accomplished up to that point: "We all agree that U.S. involvement in Southeast Asia was a mistake, but we disagree on what steps could have been taken to avoid it. Is that right?" In order for students themselves ultimately to assume responsibility for pointing out relationships between ideas, modeling by the teacher in the early stages of group development is a good way to demonstrate what kind of behavior is helpful in this regard.

STRUCTURED EXPERIENCES FOR ESTABLISH-ING NORM #2: RESPONDING TO OTHERS

In addition to observing a teacher who models good listening and responding skills, it is important for students to have direct practice in how to listen carefully and how to respond to others in classroom activities. The following structured experiences can be used to teach these skills:

1. Demonstration of Active Listening.

Conduct a demonstration of active listening, with a student volunteer as the Speaker and yourself as the Listener. Have the Speaker talk about a fairly significant personal issue or choose a controversial topic. You might wish to do "before" and "after" demonstrations to illustrate both poor listening and good listening.

After the demonstration, elicit from students a list of techniques for good listening. Make sure the following points are included:

(1) Maintain eye contact with the speaker.

(2) Signal that you're listening by saying "uh-huh" and nodding your head.

(3) Do not initially express your agreement or disagreement. Show simply that you've understood what the speaker is saying.

(4) Sit out pauses to encourage the speaker to resume talking. Don't rush to fill silences.

(5) Don't take the focus of the conversation away from the speaker by disagreeing or by talking about yourself.

(6) Use open-ended questions to encourage the speaker to continue talking or to elaborate.

(7) Summarize or restate the speaker's remarks from time to time to show that you've understood.

(8) Respond to the feelings that may lie behind the speaker's words. Show that you understand how the speaker *feels*.

2. Active Listening to One Other Person.

Divide the class into groups of three. Designate one person in each trio as Speaker, another as Listener and the third as Watchdog. Give the Speakers a choice of subjects to talk about. They may tell the Listeners something that is personally meaningful to them—for example, something that they like about themselves, something that they would like to change about themselves, something that recently happened that upset them or made them happy, a personal problem, or something important about themselves that the particular Listener doesn't already know. Or the Speakers can give their opinion on an issue, such as "What can teachers and students do to get along better with one another?" or "Does a person have to get married in order to be completely happy?"

The job of the Speakers is to explore their feelings, their thoughts, and the facts concerning the topic they have chosen. The Listeners are to practice the techniques of active listening. The Watchdogs make sure the Listeners do not violate the principles of active listening. Make it clear that the Watchdogs are not to participate in the discussion, except to point out when a Listener is not following the rules. Instruct the Watchdogs to observe the discussion carefully, withholding any suggestions for improvement until time is called.

After about five or ten minutes, call time and have the trios discuss questions such as:

> Did the Speakers really try to explore their ideas and feelings about the topic?

> Did the Listeners help the Speakers, or did they interrupt, disagree, or discourage the Speakers?

> How could the Listeners have done better?

> Did the Watchdogs keep the Listeners following the rules?

Keeping the same groups of three but changing the roles of the members within the groups, repeat the same procedure two more times so that each member of the trio has had a chance to function as Speaker, Listener and Watchdog.

3. Active Listening in a Group.

Arrange the class in one large circle (or in several smaller circles) and assign for discussion a subject-matter topic or some controversial issue such as "On what should a person base decisions about what's right and wrong?" or "What is the best way for parents to punish a child?" Instruct the students to utilize the techniques of active listening developed previously (see list, page 132) whenever a group member contributes to the discussion. That is, a person who wishes to contribute to the discussion becomes the "focus" of the discussion and the other students listen actively, responding to the speaker affirmatively as long as that person wishes to remain the "focus." Listening members should be cautioned to refrain from arguing, disagreeing, being inattentive, failing to look at the speaker, or otherwise shifting the focus away from the speaker. When the speaker is ready to relinquish the focus, another member can become the speaker and the group members listen carefully to that person.

After about ten or 15 minutes, call time and have the group discuss such questions as:

> Was it harder to listen in a group discussion than in a one-to-one conversation? Why?

> How did your behavior in this discussion differ from your usual behavior in group discussions?

> What are the advantages (or disadvantages) of stopping yourself from interrupting a speaker in order to make your own contribution?

4. People Machine.

This activity uses a non-verbal exercise to demonstrate how group members can link their contributions into an integrated working unit, with individuals responding to one another rather than operating autonomously. Push the desks back to form a large open area. Have the students stand in a circle around the edge of the open area. Instruct them to construct one huge "machine" together, using only their own bodies. Have one person start by initiating a repetitious movement, such as moving one arm up and down rhythmically, accompanying this action with a distinctive sound. Have the others join in one by one, attaching themselves in some way to someone who is already a part of the machine, adding their own movements and sounds. Continue until the entire group is interconnected and moving in many inter-related ways, making many sounds. Then stop the group and ask members what similarities they perceive between the "people machine" and an effective learning group.

5. Group Story Telling.

Seat the group in a circle. Have one student start telling a made-up story, giving only the first sentence. Ask for a volunteer, or begin the story by supplying the first sentence yourself. Then going clockwise around the circle, have each person add one new sentence to the story. Encourage students to preserve the continuity of the story and try to make it sound as much as possible as if one person had made it all up.

After students have finished, explain that this activity was designed to give them practice in linking new ideas to previous contributions. Ask them whether they had any difficulty making the connection between the previous ideas and the new one they wanted to add. Point out how important it was that they listen carefully to the previous speakers in order to perceive what direction the story was taking.

6. Responding to the Previous Speaker.

Arrange the class in one large circle. Give students a question to discuss, either a subject-matter topic or a contro-versial issue, such as "What decisions should persons your age be allowed to make for themselves and which should they not be allowed to make?" Tell students that each person can contribute only by responding in some way to the previous speaker. In other words, rather than simply stating their own position on the question, they must comment on or add to the previous contribution. Require students to look directly at the last contributor as they link their comments to what has previously been said.

If students do not have the skill or maturity to follow this procedure on their own while making their contributions in random order, you may wish to add some structure by calling on students to contribute as follows:

> a) Call on a student to give some views on the question.
>
> b) Then ask for a volunteer to respond to the first student. This speaker must look directly at the first speaker and comment on or reply to that person's remarks. Then the volunteer may add any new ideas.
>
> c) When the second speaker has finished, call for another volunteer to respond to the first or second speaker by looking directly at one of them and commenting on that person's remarks before adding new ideas.
>
> d) Continue until every group member who wishes to has contributed.

Here's Janet's recorded reaction to this activity from her personal journal:

> *The next time instead of just throwing out our opinions without thinking or commenting on others' ideas, we had to listen to what was being said before and look straight at the person. It was more uncomfortable, but the discussion had a purpose.*

7. Practice in Restating.

Move back the desks so as to form a clear path from one side of the classroom to the other. Propose some controversial issue, such as: "Should any woman be allowed to have an abortion if it is medically safe?" or "Should girls be allowed to play on varsity football teams?" or "Should homosexuals be allowed to legally marry members of the same sex?," or anything highly controversial that is appropriate for your class. Designate one wall as representing one extreme end of the issue and the opposite wall as representing the other extreme. Ask students to indicate their position on the issue by forming a continuum across the room between the two walls.

Then divide the line of students roughly into thirds— one third who have taken a more or less positive position on the issue, the middle third who are uncertain or uncommitted, and one third with a more or less negative position on the issue. Form trios by putting together one student from each of the three groups. Instruct the two students who took the pro and con positions to sit facing one another. Instruct the fairly neutral person to sit to the side to observe the interaction of the other two. Then give the following directions: "The two of you facing one another are to discuss this issue, each attempting to change the other's mind. You may use any arguments you wish to try to persuade the other person, but you must observe this one rule: before making your own statement, you must summarize the other person's remarks to his or her satisfaction. Only then may you point out how or why you disagree. In other words, you will take turns speaking, but first you must summarize what the other person said. The speaker must be satisfied with your summary before you present your rebuttal. The observer will watch to make sure you follow the rule." Instruct the observers to interrupt any person who attempts to speak without first summarizing the views of the person who spoke previously, and to make sure that the speaker is satisfied with the summary. You may wish to demonstrate the summarizing procedure with a student volunteer before setting the trios to work.

After 10 or 15 minutes, call time and discuss what took place. Call on several of the observers to tell what they saw happening, and ask the speakers what effect the summarizing procedure had on their discussion. Repeat the procedure using other topics, so that students who served as observers will have a chance to be speakers.

8. Practicing Restating in Groups.

Arrange the class in a circle (either as a total group or in small groups) and assign a controversial issue to be discussed. Require that students summarize the previous speaker's remarks before adding their own contributions. Appoint one or two students to monitor the discussions and interrupt any students who do not satisfactorily summarize the previous contribution before adding their own.

9. Practice in Perceiving Similarities and Differences.

Seat the class in a circle, and ask an open-ended subject-matter question or present a controversial issue. Ask students to volunteer to express their opinions. After three students have presented their ideas, ask for another student to volunteer to summarize the differences and similarities between the positions expressed. Then allow the discussion to continue and after three more students have spoken, once again call for someone to volunteer to explain the similarities and differences between the opinions expressed.

Once students master this procedure you can relax the structure and instead of stopping the discussion regularly, interrupt the group periodically to call for students to summarize the similarities and differences between the positions expressed by different members of the group.

10. Commercially Prepared Materials for Empathy Training.

The teacher may find some useful ideas in various commercially produced materials for teaching people to tune in and respond to the feelings of others in a way that shows them that they have been heard. The *Tune In*[2] package, for example, provides a systematic way to teach group members the skills of active listening.

The norm focused on in this chapter (responding to others) is not only an important ingredient for effective group functioning, but an invaluable asset for personal growth. Learning how to be an active listener and to respond to what a person is saying, as well as to the feelings implicit in the statement, is an extremely important social skill. Students will find that the practice they receive through the activities suggested here will carry over into their out-of-school relationships and interactions.

---

[2]*Tune In*, Listening Group, Box 3214, Milwaukee, Wisconsin 53208.

5 STAGE TWO: ESTABLISHING NORMS GOAL THREE: COOPERATION

In an effective classroom group, members work together collaboratively rather than competing against one another. Students help one another, share information and resources, provide support and suggestions—rather than trying to outstrip and outshine one another. Students in an effective group have learned that when groups work together cooperatively on a project or task the results are usually superior to those of individuals working alone.

The value of cooperation to the success of a group has been supported in the work of a number of highly respected researchers in sociology, psychology, and anthropology. One of the best known is a study by Morton Deutsch.[1] Deutsch told some classroom groups that their grades for the course would be based on the overall quality of class discussions and that every member would be given the same grade, which would

---

[1]Deutsch, Morton. An experimental study of the effects of cooperation and competition upon group process. *Human Relations*, 2 (1949), 199-231.

be indicative of how the group as a whole performed. This was the *cooperative* situation.

Other classroom groups were identical to the cooperative groups in the type of students they contained and the subject matter studied. Deutsch told these students that their grades would be based on their individual contributions in comparison to those of the other members of the group. This was the *competitive* situation. Thus, in the cooperative situation the individual earned a good grade when the whole class worked together well; in the competitive situation the individual had to outshine others in order to earn a good grade.

Deutsch found that the students in the cooperative situation produced better work and felt better about the experience than those in the competitive situation. The cooperative groups generated more and better ideas in their discussions than did the competitive groups. Students in the cooperative groups communicated with one another more effectively than those in the competitive groups; that is, in the cooperative groups the members took into account the contributions of others when making their own comments. Members of the cooperative groups were friendlier to one another, liked one another better, and made attempts to encourage other members to contribute; whereas in the competitive situation students devoted their energy to dominating and outstripping one another. Further, students in the cooperative situation were more orderly and more attentive to one another. The results clearly favored the cooperative situation.

Hammond and Goldman,[2] in a study that attempted to replicate and extend the findings of Deutsch, found that when rewards were given to a group as a whole with no competition involved, the results (in terms of involvement, attentiveness, as

---

[2]Hammond, Lee Keith, and Morton Goldman. Competition and noncompetition and its relationship to individual and group productivity. *Sociometry*, 24 (1961), 46-60.

well as performance) were superior to those obtained in situations in which rewards were given on a competitive basis.

Sherif[3] demonstrated in his experiment at Robber's Cave boys' camp that cohesiveness is increased in situations requiring cooperation. Sherif assigned the 11- and 12-year-old boys at the camp to two groups, the Rattlers and the Eagles, for a tournament of competitive games of baseball, football, and a tug of war. At first the boys were good sports, but soon the groups became angry with each other, accused each other of cheating, called one another names and one group would have nothing to do with members of the other group. They made threatening posters and raided each other's cabins; collected green apples to use as ammunition against each other. One day when the Eagles lost a game, they burned the Rattlers' banner. Changes occurred within the groups, too. One boy who had previously been considered a bully became a hero when his group had an outside "enemy." The two groups continued to be enemies even after the tournament.

Attempting to reduce the conflicts caused by competition, Sherif brought the Rattlers and Eagles together for social events. They saw movies together and started eating meals together. But the two groups continued their hostile behavior. In the dining hall, they would fight over who would get fed first. They hurled food, paper, and epithets at one another.

Sherif had the boys attend religious services in which the minister talked about brotherly love. The boys sat through the sermon, then left the church calling each other names and plotting more tricks to play on the other group.

Finally, Sherif attempted to reduce the conflicts by putting both groups into situations that would force them to cooperate with one another. He deliberately broke the water line that supplied the camp, and called all the boys together to tell them about the problem. Both Rattlers and Eagles volun-

---

[3]Sherif, Muzafer. Superordinate goals in the reduction of intergroup conflict. *American Journal of Sociology*, 63 (1956), 349-356.

teered to look for the trouble, and after a full afternoon of working together they found and fixed it.

A few days later all the boys went on a trip to a lake. When everyone was hungry, the truck which was to go into town to bring food broke down (thanks to the connivance of the camp staff). The boys found a rope and pulled together to start the truck.

Both times while the boys worked together they forgot their hostility, but as soon as the job was over the groups began quarreling again. However, after a series of situations in which everyone was forced to work together, the boys' behavior began to change. They stopped shoving on the meal lines and even began sitting together. Friendships developed between members of the two groups. The Eagles and the Rattlers held joint campfires and presented skits and songs for each other.

Sherif repeated this experiment two more times at different camps. Each time the same thing happened. When the two groups competed against each other, they became enemies and began to dislike each other. When they were brought together for social events, they continued to fight and mistreat each other. But when they were forced to cooperate on a job that they all realized was important, they gradually became friends.

Anthropologist Ruth Benedict[4] discovered, in comparing many different societies, that aggression is lowest in those social orders in which "the individual by the same act and at the same time serves his own advantage and that of the group". That is, some societies are organized so that the group values and rewards the individual for doing what benefits the group. For example, in one Eskimo society, a man proves his prowess by hunting and bringing back seals, which are then distributed equally to all members of the group for food. Thus the society benefits from the same act that benefits the individual.

---

[4]Benedict, Ruth. "Patterns of the Good Culture." *Psychology Today* (June, 1970), 53.

A society that is organized so that the individual can get ahead (accumulate wealth or power) only at the expense of the group is more likely, according to Benedict, to produce aggression. "Nonaggression occurs," she said, "not because people are unselfish and put social obligations above personal desires, but when social arrangements make the two identical." She called this quality of combining the efforts of the individual to advance the interests of the group *synergy*, a word which means that the combined action of a number of things produces results greater than the sum of the separate actions.

Creating a synergistic classroom requires that traditional classroom norms be changed. Instead of rewarding students for individual achievements, we must place a premium on cooperation and interdependence. This implies reorganization of certain classroom procedures, for example those related to grading. Since schools have imbued most students with deeply ingrained habits of competition, deliberate steps may be necessary to demonstrate to them the advantages of cooperation.

HELPFUL TEACHER BEHAVIOR FOR ESTABLISHING NORM #3: COOPERATION

Teachers, no less than students, have been conditioned to regard competition as a necessary and desirable motivating force. Teachers who would like to foster a more cooperative classroom atmosphere will have to monitor their own behavior carefully and restructure some of their classroom routines. The following practical suggestions may be helpful.

Structure learning experiences with goals that the individual student cannot meet by working alone.

The activities described previously for fostering group-centered interaction are based on this model. The goal is to demonstrate that each person in the group has something essential to contribute, and the group cannot be successful without the help of everyone. The *Mystery Game* format (see page 89) is an excellent example of this kind of learning experience.

Cooperation is also fostered by classroom activities that do not require the same performance from all students but allow students to contribute according to their particular talents or abilities. For example, an ideal classroom project would be one in which the students who are mechanically inclined can build equipment the group needs, and socially inclined team members interview people in the community, while the more verbal students research and write the group's report.

The ultimate goal is for the group members to arrive at this diversification of roles on their own—looking at their task, deciding what different things need to be accomplished, and asking themselves who in the group can best handle each different role. As an intermediate step, you may help them organize themselves for the diversification of roles by indicating the various jobs that will need to be done in order for the group to accomplish its task.

Reward cooperative rather than competitive behavior.

The research of Deutsch, and of Hammond and Goldman, indicates that changing grading procedures to reward cooperation can bring about important changes in a group. Giving all members of a group (either the total classroom group or a small learning team) the same grade based on the overall accomplishment of the group, rather than giving different grades to group members based on their differential contributions, has been shown to improve the quality of the students' work as well as their feelings about one another.

Here is an example of how I incorporate cooperative grading into a college course I teach. Each student's grade in the course is the average of the following four factors:

(1) The average of the grades that the student receives on the short quizzes given at the beginning of each class which cover the reading assignment and material introduced during the previous class.

(2) The average of the grades all members of the class receive on all these quizzes.

(3) The grade the group achieves on the final exam, which will be a group task, a problem which will require all students to apply what they've learned in the course.

(4) The grade I give each student for the degree to which he or she has helped the class meet its goal, which is "for every member to learn as much as possible about group dynamics."

In this course I have two students whom I taught in previous courses which were not graded cooperatively. It has been interesting to observe the changes cooperative grading has brought about in the behavior of these two students. In the previous class, Marsha was both highly motivated and capable, the typical outstanding student. She worked very hard, contributed well, though not too frequently, to class discussions, wrote an excellent term paper, and made the top grade on the final exam. Don, on the other hand, was one of the poorest students in the course. He was likeable enough, but seemed willing to get by with a minimum of effort. His semester grade was a D, and considering how little he learned perhaps even that was a bit generous.

Marsha and Don's reactions to the new grading system were very interesting. Marsha squirmed a little, probably because she had been used to making A's through individual effort, and worried that the new system would penalize her since she didn't like to get too involved with other people. Don was hopeful that the new procedure would help him get a higher grade than otherwise, but he was also a bit nervous that other people might resent him for pulling down the group's average. Gradually Marsha began to overcome her shyness about interacting with others, since to get a good grade she had to help the other members make a good grade also. But even more exciting was the change in Don; to avoid pulling down the group's average, he began working hard and taking an active role in classroom activities.

Several high school teachers I know have applied the principle of group grading in their classes. A math teacher, for example, divides his class into learning teams of five students each. He announces that they are to work together on all practice exercises and that every member of the team is responsible for making sure that all other members understand the material thoroughly. At the end of each unit, he administers a quiz to check their progress and gives all members of each team the average grade of the members of their team.

An English teacher doing a unit on composition devised an ingenious technique for applying principles of cooperation to the highly individualized process of developing writing skills. She assigned students at random to learning teams of approximately four students each. Each student on the team wrote a composition which was carefully examined by the other members of the team to see if the ideas were stated as clearly and correctly as possible. They made suggestions for improving the composition, but did not edit or revise a team member's work. The student who wrote the paragraph revised it in accordance with their suggestions and submitted it to the teacher. The teacher graded each member of the team by averaging the scores of all the members' compositions. Thus, to assure that they all got high grades, the more talented students had to help less able team members improve their work. This teacher reports that students are improving their skills far quicker when coached by teammates than they had when *she* marked the errors.

Make sure individual needs are met through behavior that contributes to group goals.

Grading based on the accomplishment of the entire group rather than on individual performance is likely to produce considerable anxiety in high achieving students, anxiety which usually shows itself in cries of "That's not fair! Why should I work hard and have my grade brought down by some dummy?!" It's not hard to understand these students because, for many of them, earning higher grades than other students has been their only way of achieving recognition and status. I, myself, understand their concern, because in high school earning high grades was very important to me: I had few other ways of getting approval and recognition. I was not as charming and handsome as Sammy Waggener, nor as athletic as Butch Beverly, nor as outgoing as David Duncan. Just about all I had going for me was my ability to make good grades, and to be placed in a class in which everyone got the same grade would have disturbed me considerably.

Alternative means should be provided for such people—ways, as Ruth Benedict suggests, that give them personal approval and at the same time further the goals of the total group. Thus, they may gain recognition and admiration from the group by taking leadership roles in the learning team, by making contributions to the team's progress, and by helping slower students improve their skills and thus raise the group's average grade.

Changing a student's relationship with others from competition to cooperation can have a profound and lasting effect. In my senior year in high school, when I was breezing through English 12, I was restless and bored. In the same class languished seven students whose grades in English 12 were so low that they might fail to graduate from high school that year. Sensing my boredom and wishing to do everything possible to help those seven students make it through English and graduation, Mrs. Wiles (that's her real name) suggested that I meet with the seven each day during our study hall period to tutor them. She provided me with extra materials, including teacher's manuals, and turned me loose, requiring only that I do my best to help them pass English 12.

My self-concept got quite a boost from this new role, but even more important was the effect it had on my relationship with those seven students, most of whom I had rarely spoken to in other classes. We were thrown together with a common purpose to which we were all highly committed—they, because their graduation depended on it; I, because my ego depended on it.

At first our interaction was stiff and awkward. I wasn't sure they'd like having me work with them, and I suppose they weren't too eager to show off their stupidity in front of a successful student. But over the weeks we got to know each other and started enjoying our work together. My feelings about "dummies" changed drastically, and I suppose their feelings about me changed too, because on the night of graduation—when all seven of my charges were ready to march into the auditorium—they took me aside, mumbled their gratitude, and handed me a thank-you present (a white Oxford-cloth shirt that I've never thrown away, despite its frayed collar and cuffs). Looking back, I think I probably learned more than they did!

The first step in creating a classroom environment in which students can meet their own needs while contributing to the welfare of the group is to determine what kinds of goals individual students might have. Most students want approval from the teacher and the respect and approval of fellow students. They want to find answers to things they are curious about; to develop certain skills they perceive as personally important; and to earn grades which are symbols of status, prestige, and accomplishment.

In different schools students may be motivated by different needs and goals. In the affluent suburban high school where I taught, grades were very important because most students were eager to get into a prestige university, whereas in the inner-city school where my wife was teaching, students' needs centered on obtaining good jobs so they could improve their economic status. And, of course, even within the same class, individual needs and goals vary widely. Some students desperately need good grades to please their parents, and others care only about peer group acceptance.

The next step is to determine what the specific goals of the class are; that is, what the group is trying to achieve. For example, the goal might be for everyone to know how to divide complex fractions, or to find out all they can about earthworms, or for everyone to know how to write an expository paragraph, or to understand the provisions of the Bill of Rights.

Now you can organize methods for achieving the goals of the classroom group which, at the same time, meet the goals of individual members. For example, a student who has sought to gain peer group recognition by monopolizing class discussions may find that helping other members of the group learn about fractions (or earthworms or the Bill of Rights) wins greater approval than did showing off how much one knows oneself.

Encourage students' natural impulses to cooperate.

Although the norm of competition is inculcated in most American students beginning as early as first grade, most students do have impulses to help one another. Much of what is labelled "cheating" by teachers is actually a healthy impulse to help someone else. Not that cheating should be condoned, but too often, in our urgency to put an end to dishonesty, we stifle helpful behavior as well. The following example is not atypical. Margy, a student teacher, had spent several minutes explaining a math concept at the board, and then assigned a fairly complex problem for the students to work at individually. A number of students were having trouble with the problem, so Margy walked down the row of desks, helping them one at a time. Meanwhile, some of the students spon-taneously turned around or leaned across the aisle to offer suggestions to others who hadn't yet mastered the problem. When Margy became aware of this she spoke sharply to the class: "Turn around and do your own work. If you've finished, sit quietly in your seat. If you need help, raise your hand and I'll come help you." Students got the message clearly enough—"If you help one another, that's bad. I'm the only one here who can help you." Not only did Margy discourage students' healthy tendency to cooperate, but from a purely practical standpoint she was defeating herself, since there was simply not enough time for her to get around to every student who needed help. She could have made valuable use of the help the students volunteered to offer.

By contrast, another student teacher, Jim, was very comfortable with students' working together on individual tasks. He taught an inquiry-oriented seventh-grade science course in which students spent most of their time working individually on short investigations from which they drew conclusions. Some students preferred to work alone on the investigations, following the instructions and asking the teach-er for help when they had questions. But others very naturally and spontaneously teamed up or formed small groups and worked cooperatively. Jim quietly checked to make sure all students were understanding the principles and kept his eye on the teams and small groups to make sure the abler kids weren't just handing answers out to the slower ones. But he recognized the value of letting students work together and seemed to believe that it benefited rather than harmed their learning.

As a teacher trying to establish the norm of cooperation in your classroom, you must monitor your behavior carefully to make sure you don't automatically or unconsciously dis-courage students from helping one another. This requires that you think through carefully whether you want students to talk to one another or whether you consider this disruptive behavior.

It's useful to discuss with students what constitutes helping another person, so they can distinguish between just giving the answer and really helping the other person understand how to arrive at the answer. I sometimes quote the old saying, "Give a man a fish, and he'll be hungry again tomorrow. But teach him how to catch his own fish, and he'll never be hungry again." You might want to spend some time teaching students how to be teachers for one another—how to explain a process, how to lead a person inductively to a conclusion, how to provide practice with a concept. Give the class specific opportunities to practice teaching things to one another. For older students, the unit on "Helping" in *Becoming: A Course in Human Relations*[5] provides a valuable introduction to what is and what is not helpful helping.

STRUCTURED EXPERIENCES FOR ESTABLISHING NORM #3: COOPERATION

It may be useful to start by letting students experiment in observing their own behavior in an activity that requires cooperation, or in which the differences between cooperative and competitive behavior are made graphically apparent. Thus the first activities suggested here are mostly for "consciousness raising" purposes rather than skill training.

1. Broken Squares.

This activity requires that the class be divided into small groups of five or six persons each. Each small group will receive a set of five envelopes containing puzzle pieces cut into

---

[5]Chester R. Cromwell, William Ohs, Albert E. Roark, Gene Stanford. *Becoming: A Course in Human Relations*, Philadelphia, Pa.: J.B. Lippincott Co., 1975.

shapes that they will have to form into five 6″ x 6″ squares as in the diagram below:

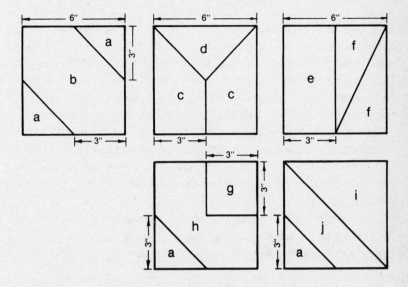

To prepare one puzzle set, cut out five cardboard squares, 6″ x 6″, then draw the lines as indicated in the diagram. Pencil the letters lightly on the pieces. Then cut each square apart on the internal lines and put the pieces into five envelopes as follows: In envelope 1 place pieces *i*, *h*, and *e*; in envelope 2 place pieces *a*, *a*, *a*, and *c*; in envelope 3 place pieces *a* and *j*; in envelope 4 place pieces *d* and *f*; in envelope 5 place pieces *g*, *b*, *f*, and *c*. Erase the letters and on each puzzle piece write the number of the envelope in which it has been placed. This will facilitate returning the pieces to the proper envelope after the activity. Prepare enough puzzle sets so that each small group has a complete set of five puzzles.

Have the small groups work at tables or on the floor so that they have a flat playing surface before them. If a group has more than five members, have the group decide which five will actually do the task and who will serve as observers.

Instruct the five workers to form a tight circle, with the observers sitting outside the circle.

Give the following instructions: "Working in your small groups, I want you to put together a puzzle, but it's not as simple as it may sound. I am handing each of you an envelope that contains puzzle pieces. Take the pieces out of the envelopes and put them on the table (floor) in front of you. Please do not pick them up until I signal you to begin work. Distributed among the five of you are puzzle pieces that will form five complete squares of equal dimensions. I want each of you to assemble one square in front of you. The task is not complete until each person in the group has formed a complete square with all squares being the same size. You may exchange puzzle pieces if you wish, *but no member may speak*. You may not ask for a puzzle piece that another member has; you must wait until that member gives it to you. You must observe the following rules while putting together your puzzles, and the observers have the job of strictly enforcing these rules:

(1) Each of you must construct a square on the table (or floor) directly in front of yourself.

(2) You may not ask for a piece from any other person. This means no talking, gesturing, motioning, or signaling in any other way that you want to get a piece from another member of your group. The only way you can get a piece from another person is for that person to give it to you.

(3) You may pass any of your pieces to any other group member at any time.

(4) No member is to talk at any time. The only person who can talk is the observer, who can interrupt only to stop a violation of the rules. The observer may not make suggestions to the players."

After asking if students have any questions about the procedure, have them begin to work. Note that it will be possible for *some* of the participants to form complete squares before all the others are finished, but only if the proper combinations are arrived at will it be possible for *all five* participants to complete their squares. Often, students who have completed their squares will not consider that an alternative combination might result in *all* members completing their squares, and will refuse to break up their squares and pass pieces to other members.

After the groups have finished the task (or after about 15 minutes), conduct a discussion of the activity. Encourage students to talk about the difficulties they encountered and the strategies they used to overcome them. Ask them what they discovered about cooperation—what attitudes and behaviors cooperation requires that are different from those competition demands. Pose questions such as:

> How did you feel when someone had a piece someone else needed and didn't pass it to the other person?

> How did you feel when someone completed a square and then sat back without considering that this solution may have prevented others from finishing their squares?

> How did you feel if you finished your square and then realized you might have to break it up and give away pieces in order to help others?

> How could you apply what you learned in this activity to other classroom group projects?

2. Scrambled Sentences.

Instead of, or as a follow-up to the activity above, give the small groups sets of cards on which words have been printed. Follow the same directions, having each person in the group form a meaningful sentence. To prepare the materials write one word on a card and place words in envelopes as follows:

Envelope 1 contains: *Spring, begun, eager, into*
Envelope 2 contains: *here, blinded, have, dashed, the*
Envelope 3 contains: *is, The, start, reading, The*
Envelope 4 contains: *sunlight, barking, I'm, cat, house*
Envelope 5 contains: *The, me, dogs, to*

Give instructions similar to those for *Broken Squares*. Point out that the first word in the sentences have been capitalized as a clue. The unscrambled sentences are:

Spring is here.

The sunlight blinded me.

The dogs have begun barking.

I'm eager to start reading.

The cat dashed into the house.

It may be possible to form other meaningful sentences with these words, so do not require students to arrive at exactly these sentences. The only requirement is that each member of the group complete a sentence that is grammatically and syntactically correct.

3. Earn As Many Points As You Can.

Divide the group into trios, and designate one person in each group to be Blue, a second person to be White, and the third person to be the scorekeeper. Instruct the Blue and White players to sit back to back, so that they cannot see each other. Give each of them a 3″ x 5″ card with X on one side and Y on the reverse side. Explain that the game will be played in rounds. During each round, Blue and White will each choose to show the scorekeeper either the X or the Y side of their index card. The players will earn different numbers of points depending on what decisions they both make. To explain the scoring procedure, put the following chart on the board:

BLUE

	X	Y
X	B=+5 W=+5	B=+10 W=-10
Y	B=-10 W=+10	B=-5 W=-5

If both choose X, each earns five points.

If both choose Y, each loses five points.

If White chooses X and Blue chooses Y, White loses 10 points and Blue gains 10 points.

If White chooses Y and Blue chooses X, White gains 10 points and Blue loses 10 points.

Announce that the goal of the game is *to earn as many points as possible*. After stating this, write it on the board so that you can refer to it later. Sometimes, because they are in the habit of competing, students mistakenly assume that the goal is to make more points than the other player, regardless of how high or low the scores may be. This is *not* the goal, but do not go into an explanation or try to disabuse students of their misconception until *after* they have played the game. Simply announce the purpose clearly and write it on the board. If the players distort your message and compete, each trying to get a higher score than the other instead of working together so that both might achieve the highest possible score, you can discuss it as part of the follow-up discussion.

Players may not consult with each other. The score-keeper must strictly enforce the *no talking* rule. For each round, the players simultaneously show their scorekeeper the side of the index card that indicates their decision. The scorekeeper then announces how both players voted and records the score they each earned on the scorecard.

SCORE CARD

Name of Player	1	2	3	4
BLUE ( )				
WHITE ( )				

Play at least 10 rounds before stopping to discuss the activity. Raise questions such as these in the follow-up discussion:

How did you feel toward the other player during the game?

What strategy did you use to increase your score?

What strategy did the other player use?

Find out which players made the highest scores in the class and ask them to explain their strategies. Lead the class to examine whether a cooperative strategy (both players choosing X most of the time) or a competitive strategy (choosing Y in hopes the other player would choose X) led to a higher score. Broaden the discussion to a general consideration of whether cooperation or competition leads toward greater outcomes for both persons.

Two alternative structures are possible in playing this game. One is to divide the class into two groups and have one group be the White team and the other the Blue team. Members of each team talk over what choice they want to make as a group on each round. They report their decision

5	6	7	8	9	10	Total

secretly to the teacher, who serves as scorekeeper. This format requires that each group be situated in such a way as not to overhear the discussion of the other group. It also requires more time, since for each round the group members must come to a decision after deliberation among themselves.

A second alternate format is to have two volunteers play the game while the rest of the class watches. The volunteers sit back to back at the front of the classroom and show their choices to the teacher, who serves as scorekeeper. This procedure, while more orderly than the others, does not confront every student with a choice between cooperative and competitive behavior.

This activity lends itself to many different subject-matter applications. For example, the game could be used to explore the possibilities for cooperation versus conflict between oil-producing nations and manufacturing nations that sell goods to the oil-producing nations. One player represents the oil-producing nations and chooses whether or not to raise the price of oil. The other player represents the manufacturing nations (including the U.S.) and decides whether or not to raise the price of the goods they sell to the oil producers. Both the oil producers and the manufacturers want to make as much money for themselves as they can, and the question is what is the best way for both sides to achieve their goal.

Put the following scoring diagram on the board:

OIL PRODUCERS

	HOLD	RAISE
MANUFACTURERS HOLD	OP +5 M +5	OP +10 M -10
MANUFACTURERS RAISE	OP -10 M +10	OP -5 M -5

If both groups hold their prices at present levels they will both make a profit (+5). If both raise their prices, they will both lose (-5) because of the resulting inflation. The way for either side to make the largest profit is for one to raise prices while the other group holds prices, but how long will the group that holds prices tolerate losing money?

After the game is played the follow-up questions might include: What have you learned from this game about how the manufacturing nations and the oil-producing nations can best deal with one another?

Countless other international situations could be investigated using this same model, such as: the Russia/USA arms race, the Cuban missile crisis, relations between the U.S. and China.

4. Commercial Game Materials.

William Nesbitt has adapted this format for an activity entitled "The Oil Island Dispute," which is described in *Teaching Youth About Conflict and War*, National Council for the Social Studies, Washington, D.C., 1973. Still another adaptation entitled "Dilemma of the Tribes" appears in *Experiences in Inquiry*, Association of American Geographers and the American Sociological Association, Allyn and Bacon, 1974.

Interesting but somewhat more complex variations of the game appear in other publications: "Win As Much As You Can," in *A Handbook of Structured Experiences for Human Relations Training*, Vol. II, by Pfeiffer and Jones; and "The Game of Life" in Elizabeth Hunter's *Encounter in the Classroom*, Holt, 1972.

The Road Game by Thomas E. Linehan and Barbara Ellis Long, Herder & Herder, N.Y., is a fascinating activity that combines art and social studies and focuses on issues of cooperation and competition. Players are required to trace a road through territory that belongs to other teams, causing conflicts that can lead to cooperation or chaos.

5. Write On—A Scenario for Poetry.

Allan A. Glatthorn[6] has devised a structured approach for assigning an interdependent small group task. He specifies what roles need to be filled, what skills the person selected should have, and what the person in that role should do at each step in the process of completing the task. An adaptation of one of his assignment packets dividing the class into groups of five is given below. Interestingly enough, it approaches the writing of poetry—generally assumed to be an individual task—as a small group task. His structure could be adapted to almost any number of subject-matter topics.

WRITE ON: A SCENARIO FOR POETRY

Before We Start . . .

This is a scenario for poetry. And this scenario will help you do three things:

(1) It will help you and a few other people organize yourselves into a group so that you can work together better.

(2) It will tell you what steps you should take together in order to write a poem.

(3) It will make some suggestions to you about how you and the group can perform the poem you have written.

To Help Your Group Work Together . . .

Five people will have to play an active role. Look over the roles and skills listed below and decide which job

---

[6]Glatthorn, Allan A. *Write On: A Scenario for Poetry*. Mimeographed learning packet. No date. Reprinted with permission of the author.

you can best perform. In order to get the group moving, ask the person whose name is last alphabetically to be the head of the group during the five minutes it takes to get organized.

GROUP ROLE	JOB PERFORMED AND SKILLS NEEDED	PERSON CHOSEN
Leader	Provides leadership during activity. Is able to help the group work together; can help the group settle any differences and make decisions.	_____
Sound & Light Specialist	Chooses the right background music, sounds, and lighting effects; operates recording equipment. Should understand equipment and music.	_____
Director	Directs the group in performing the poem; can help people speak aloud more effectively. Should have some acting skill or interest.	_____
Writer	Keeps all written records; decides how the poem should look on the page. Should have sense of color, form, shape, and be able to spell.	_____
Reader	Reads all directions aloud if people have questions; reads the "mood words" and solo part. Should be able to read well.	_____

Being Scared: A Scenario on Fear

Fear is one of the strongest emotions. It therefore makes a good subject for poetry. So let's begin to write a poem about fear.

A. Setting the Mood	
Specialists' Jobs	**Everyone's Job**
(1) Leader: Be sure everyone knows what to do. (2) Sound & Light Specialist: Choose some music or some recorded sounds that suggest a mood of fear. Adjust the lighting appropriately. (3) Reader: While the music is playing, read this aloud to the group: We all are afraid—of the ghost in the night, the man in the room, the dream in our head. Sometimes the fear is right there before our eyes, and our mouths go dry and our bodies shake. But sometimes the fear is deep in the pit of our stomachs, and all we know is the ache inside. What do you fear most of all?	Close your eyes. Listen to the music and the words and try to remember the last time you felt fear. What did it feel like? What makes you most afraid? Bring back fear so it is alive again inside your head, and maybe this time you can look it in the face.

B. Writing the First Draft

Specialists' Jobs	Everyone's Job
(1) Leader: Lead the group step by step through the scenario below. Try to get the group to do one section together at a time. Be sure each person has a chance to speak, and help people listen to each other. Help the group decide which ideas they will include in their group poem. (People may do their own individual poems later on if they wish.) (2) Writer: Be sure you copy correctly the lines the group finally decides on. Don't worry about appearance now—just the right words. You are making the official copy.	Read through the scenario below and begin to think about how you would fill in the blanks to make a poem. Then share your ideas with the others, and listen to the ideas they have. Later on you may want to write your own private poem, but your job now is to help the group produce a poem together.

The Scenario—for Everyone

The questions to help you think:	Your answers—To shape a poem
What do you fear most of all?	I fear the _____

When do you know this fear? Think of three times or places, and build up to a climax by putting the worst time or place last.	I fear it _____ _____ _____
What happens to you physically or emotionally when you feel that fear?	My _____ _____
Think of a comparison that would make your reaction seem clear to the reader.	like the _____ _____
Repeat the first line.	I fear the _____
What do you do about trying to make the fear go away? How do you try to deal with it?	So I _____ _____
And then what happens to that fear? Does it go away, become worse, or just go deeper inside you?	And the fear _____ _____
Write a one-sentence concluding line, or repeat the first line again.	_____

C. Writing the Final Draft

Specialists' Jobs	Everyone's Job
(1) Leader: Help the group review the first draft and make suggestions about improving it. (2) Writer: Make an accurate copy of the revised draft. Then, with the help of the group, write the final poem on a large sheet of paper, paying special attention to how the poem looks on the page. Space out the words and lines so that the use of space fits the sense of the words. Use different forms and shapes of letters to call attention to key words. Make the written poem a thing of visual beauty.	(1) Work together to revise the poem. Pay special attention to the sounds of words (does the sound fit the sense?), the use of words (does each word say exactly what you want it to say?), the use of comparisons (does the comparison seem original and does it suggest the idea intended?) (2) Help the writer make the visual presentation beautiful.

D. Performing the Poem

Specialists' Jobs	Everyone's Job

(1) Director: Your important job now is to help the group say the poem aloud or perform it so that the poem comes alive as an auditory experience.
 	
   a. Tell the reader which lines to speak in solo.
 	
   b. You might choose another good speaker to act as the reader's echo—to repeat a few seconds later some of the key words in that line.
 	
   c. Decide which lines the whole group should say together in chorus.
 	
   d. Help the group practice the performance once or twice; give them cues or signals as they go, pointing out which person is to speak.
 	
(2) Sound and Light Specialist: With the director's help and advice, decide which music or sound and light effects should be used during the performance. Try to use sound and light that fit the mood of the poem.
	Work together to make the poem become an exciting experience in sound.

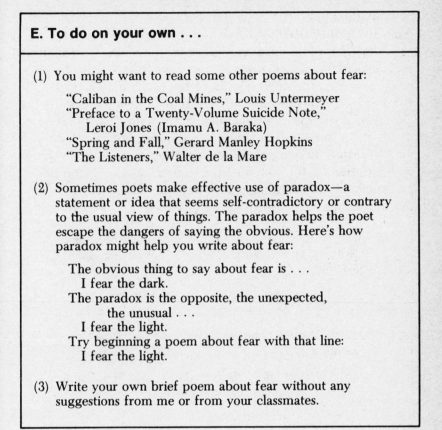

E. To do on your own . . .

(1) You might want to read some other poems about fear:

> "Caliban in the Coal Mines," Louis Untermeyer
> "Preface to a Twenty-Volume Suicide Note,"
> Leroi Jones (Imamu A. Baraka)
> "Spring and Fall," Gerard Manley Hopkins
> "The Listeners," Walter de la Mare

(2) Sometimes poets make effective use of paradox—a statement or idea that seems self-contradictory or contrary to the usual view of things. The paradox helps the poet escape the dangers of saying the obvious. Here's how paradox might help you write about fear:

> The obvious thing to say about fear is . . .
> I fear the dark.
> The paradox is the opposite, the unexpected,
> the unusual . . .
> I fear the light.
> Try beginning a poem about fear with that line:
> I fear the light.

(3) Write your own brief poem about fear without any suggestions from me or from your classmates.

6. Cooperative Games for Younger Students.[7]

Many traditional games call for some degree of cooperation. But in most games as we know them there is some team

---

[7]The material on cooperative games, which begins on page 169, was adapted from a mimeographed report compiled by Ruth Cornelius, of the St. Louis public schools, and Theodore F. Lentz, Director of the Peace Research Laboratory in St. Louis, and is used with the permission of Louise Robison on behalf of the late Mr. Lentz.

or individual to be competed against. This element is deleted from the games that follow and cooperation is the goal.

All cooperative games present a certain amount of challenge to the players because they have to deal with chance factors or with the uncertainties of the nonhuman aspects of the game; i.e., the placement or speed of a pitched or a kicked or a batted ball, the combination of cards within each player's hand, the alternatives for moves within a play, etc. Games which are designed to develop cooperative attitudes utilize the uncertainties of the nonhuman elements in the game and minimize the competition against persons. These games have the following characteristics:

a) All participants strive toward a common goal, working with each other instead of competing against each other.

b) All players win if the goal is attained, or all lose if the goal is not attained.

c) All players compete against the nonhuman elements of the game rather than against other players.

d) Players combine their different skills in a united effort to reach the common goal.

In most traditional games the goal is for individuals or teams to exercise their skills to thwart or outdo, or get a higher score than the competing individuals or teams. Since there is no one to compete against in cooperative games, new goals have to be defined and new skills developed to work together in achieving these goals. The cooperative games that are described below may be roughly classified according to five underlying features or game principles:

Simultaneous Finish—The goal is for all players to make the final move at the same time.

Coordinated Manipulation—All players attempt to coordinate their timing and movement with other group members so that a smooth pattern of manipulation results.

Rotation—Each player takes a turn in sequence and is responsible for one step or phase indispensible to the final or progressive goal.

Equal Division—Players attempt to play so that by the time the game is over, all members have achieved the same score or object.

Predetermined Score—The players make combined efforts to achieve a set score.

Game Principle I   Simultaneous Finish

Cooperative Checkers.   In cooperative checkers, the two players aim to exchange all the black checkers and all the red checkers so that they are all on opposite sides of the board from where they started. The game differs from the usual checkers rules in that there is no jumping or moving backwards, and no checkers are removed. The game is won if each player's last checker is moved to the last open position on the opposite side of the board at the same time.

Cooperative Chinese Checkers.   The goal of this game is for each player's marbles to end up in the home section at the same time. The game follows the original rules of Chinese Checkers, except that all players strive to finish the game at the same time. The players do not make identical moves, but they move each of their marbles, jump their own or others, in such a way as to be of benefit to other players. The game is won if all players can place their last marble in the home section on the last round.

Game Principle II   Coordinated Manipulation

Cooperative Three Deep.   Players form a double circle, with each player in the outer circle standing in back of a player in the inner circle. One player stands in the center of the circle. The center player throws a ball (preferably a large rubber ball or a volleyball) to any player in the inner circle. Immediately upon releasing the ball, the center player runs and stands in back of someone in the outer circle.

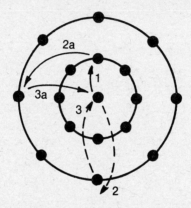

This person must run to the center in time to catch the ball that, in the meantime, has been thrown by the person in the inner circle to someone in the outer circle. The new center player catches the ball thrown by the person in the outer circle, and now throws the ball to another player in the inner circle, runs and takes a position behind a player in the outer circle, and so the game continues, with players coordinating their movements so that the new center player gets back in time to catch the ball.

Cooperative Bowling.   The goal of the game is to knock down the 10 pins in as many rounds as there are players. If three students are playing, the first person attempts to knock down some of the pins; the second attempts to knock down a few more; the third attempts to knock down the remaining pins. The order of the players can be changed for each game so as to distribute advantages and disadvantages of the first and last turns. (Some children revised this game and had all three children throw their balls at the same time, endeavoring to knock all the pins down at once.)

Tossing the Ring.   One player holds a stick. Another player, standing 15 to 20 feet from the first, tosses the ring attempting to encircle the stick, while the first player attempts to catch the ring on the stick.

Blanket Toss.   For this game you need a large sheet or blanket in which a hole big enough for a balloon to fall through has been cut. Balloons of different sizes are placed on the sheet. The players hold the sheet stretched out among them and toss the balloons up into the air by jerking the sheet. They attempt to move the sheet in such a way that all the balloons will fall through the hole. When they have finished, the players may repeat this game and time themselves to see if their skill in working together has improved.

Rein Ball.   For this game, you need to construct the following equipment: Two long ropes are joined somewhere toward the middle by two 12-inch long cross pieces of rope placed about 18 inches apart. From one of the cross pieces, suspend a tennis ball, encased in a net, from a rope 18 inches long. Two or four players play together, holding the ends of the long ropes. The object of the game is to see how many successive times they can get the ball to swing around the cross piece of rope.

Game Principle III   Rotation

Pan Pong.   Each player has a pan (a saucepan, frying pan, dishpan, or tray will do). Players form a circle. One player bounces the ball out of his or her pan into the pan of the next player. The purpose is to see how long the players can keep bouncing the ball around the circle from one pan into the next. A player needn't get the ball into the next pan in one bounce, but can keep bouncing the ball into the air until the transfer can successfully be made.

Cooperative Jacks.   The game follows the traditional procedure, except that instead of one player going through all the paces, the players take turns. That is, the first player picks up all the jacks one at a time; the second player throws them and picks up two at a time; the next, three, etc. If any player is unsuccessful in any way (touching a jack or missing the ball), the group has to begin all over again. The next player, then, begins with one; the following player with two, etc. The game is won when the group has progressed to and succeeded with sixes. (For very young children, the game can be simplified by eliminating the use of the ball, merely throwing the jacks and picking up the appropriate number in succession.)

Cooperative Jump Rope.   Two players turn the rope. The other players line up to jump. The first player jumps once, runs out and quickly takes one end of the rope. The player who had been turning goes to the end of the line. Meanwhile, the second player jumps two times, runs out, and takes the other end of the rope, relieving that player to go to the end of the line. The third player jumps three times and runs out to take one end of the rope, and so on. If a miss occurs, the next player begins all over again jumping once; the next, twice, etc.

Through the Loop.   Players stand in a line—1, 2, 3, 4, 5, 6, 7. Player 2's arms are arched over his or her head. Player 3 throws the ball to player 1, through the arched arms of 2. Player 1 catches the ball and swiftly moves to the end behind 7, giving the ball to 4 on the way. Player 4 now throws the ball to player 2 through the arched arms of player 3. Player 2 catches the ball and moves to the end of the line behind 1, giving the ball to player 5. And so the game continues.

Center Throw. Players form a circle, with one player standing in the center. The center player throws the ball to any player in the circle, and immediately runs to take the position in the circle of any other player. The displaced player runs to the center to receive the ball thrown by the player who received it from the center player. The plays thus continue.

Bouncing Ball Series. Players form a circle. The first player bounces a ball once over to the next player, who without any interruption, catches the ball and bounces it two times; the next player catches the ball on the second bounce, and bounces it to the next player on the third bounce, etc. If the ball is fumbled or missed by any player, the next player begins all over again bouncing the ball once; the next one, twice, etc.

A variation of the game is to bounce as described above once around the circle until the ball comes back to the one who started the game. This player bounces the ball one more time than the preceding player. But the next player starts over again at one. This variation prevents the bouncing from reaching such high numbers that successive players have to wait too long for their turns.

Circle Kick. Players form a circle. One player kicks a soccer ball to any player on the opposite side of the circle, calling out "One." The player receiving the ball kicks it to another part of the circle, calling "Two," and so on, each player calling out the next higher number. If the ball goes out of the circle, or if any player touches the ball instead of kicking it, the progress of the game is forfeited, and the group begins over again with "One." The object is to see how high a score the group can reach.

Game Principle IV   *Equal Division*

Equality.   The goal of this card game is that each player end with the same number of points. The cards are dealt out equally among the players. The first player leads any card and the other players follow suit. (If they cannot follow suit, they may throw any other card.) The player who has thrown the highest card (ace is highest, with king, queen, jack, 10, etc., following) takes the trick. The player who wins the trick places face up on the table any ace, 2, 3, 4, or 5 that was in the trick. All cards higher than 5 that were in the trick do not count and are discarded. This player now leads a card and the play proceeds in like manner. All the players attempt to follow suit or discard in such a way as to give the trick to the player who needs points to make all the scores equal. The scoring system is as follows: aces count one point each, twos count two points each, threes count three each, fours count four each, and fives count five each. The total number of points is 60. At the end of the game, each player's score must be the same. Thus to get the goal score, divide 60 by the number of players.

Game Principle V   *Predetermined Score*

Heaven.   In this card game all players bid on how many tricks they think they can take with their own hand. The total number of tricks bid by all players must add up to 13. The goal is for all players to attempt to fulfill their own and each other's bids. All the cards are dealt out and the first player leads any card. The highest card takes the trick. There are no trumps. A player who cannot follow suit throws off. The game is won if each player gets the number of tricks bid.

Bat Ball.   The goal of this game is for the players to score more points than are credited to the game. The game scores a point every time the ball hits the ground. The players score a point every time the batted ball is caught without touching the ground. Players form a more or less complete circle around the batter, at a distance suitable for pitching and catching. Anyone who catches or recovers the ball may either pitch to the batter or throw the ball to another player who is in a better position to pitch. Each player takes a turn at batting from one to five times. Positions are rotated at the convenience and will of the players. They may choose a regular or a variable rotation.

Half In and Half Out.   For this game you will need a three-foot-square board set on legs two inches high, and twelve wooden discs, two inches in diameter. In the center of the board is drawn a circle 10 inches in diameter; within this circle there is a hole five inches in diameter. The goal of the game is to get half the discs into the hole and, at the same time, to have the remaining discs either on the 10-inch circle line, or in the space between the circle line and the hole.

To begin the game, place six discs equidistant around the circle line. Place the remaining discs around the edges of the board to be used as shooters. Players take turns flicking one of these shooter discs, attempting to knock one of the other discs from the circle into the hole. Any disc which lands in the space between the hole and the circle ceases to be used as a shooter; any disc which lands outside the circle on the board can be re-used as a shooter. The game is won when players succeed in getting six of the discs through the hole at the same time that six of the discs are on the circle or in the space between the circle and the hole. The following are variations of the game: (1) Use more than 12 discs. (2) Before the game is begun, players agree upon their own goal—e.g., eight of the discs must go through the hole while four stay in the circle territory, etc. (3) Play the game on the floor, drawing a two-foot circle within a four-foot circle, and use discs like those used in shuffleboard.

Cooperative Shuffleboard.   The game is played as in competitive shuffleboard, except that the court is drawn to look something like this:

10	-8	-10
-5	8	7
-3	3	5

Players take turns shooting the discs into the court. The goal is to place their shots so that the combined score will total exactly 15 when all discs have been used. Actually, the usual shuffleboard court can be used merely by changing some of the numbers to minus.

Horseshoes.   Before the game, the players decide what score they will strive for with a certain number of throws. For example, four players might agree to strive for a combined total score of 80 in 40 throws (or five rounds). The scoring system is: ringer = 5 points, horseshoe landing within designated territory = 1 point. The players stand at one stake and take turns pitching toward the opposite stake. Each player pitches two horseshoes during one round. If the predetermined score is achieved with the specified number of throws, the game has been won.

Sequences.   Deal out all the cards among players (two to 10 can play the game). The goal of the game is for all players to have an entire run of numbers in consecutive order without regard to suit. Players arrange the cards in their hands. All call out a desired number simultaneously. Then all players pass one of their cards to the left. If they have the number desired by the person on the left, they pass that card. If not, they pass another that someone else has called out in hopes that it will soon reach the person who desires it. The sequence is repeated again, with all players calling out a desired number simultaneously, and everyone passing a card to the left. As soon as any players have four or more cards in sequence, they place the cards on the table in front of them, and then add other numbers as they get them. The game is won when all players have all cards in sequence. Before the game is begun, the players can agree on a specified number of turns in which they must complete their game.

Results of Cooperative Games

The rules in cooperative games are more flexible than in standard games in that the players themselves take an active part in formulating them. Play activity in cooperative games tends to be less authoritarian than in competitive activities. With no other team, side, or individual to compete against, players can agree on modifications of the procedures as the game progresses. More planning takes place in cooperative games while the game goes on. More suggestions are made by players to each other. This not only makes for more cooperation, but also produces greater creativity and inventiveness as variations and new games result.

There is less resentment about an individual's bungling a play. The group members as a whole attempt to compensate for each other's errors. When children engage in competitive games on the playground, arguments such as these are often heard: "You're out!" "I am not!" "You cheat." "You lie." "You don't know how to play." And if the quarrels get too tough, the children either come to some neutral party for a decision or the game blows up. Quarrels are fewer and much less vehement in cooperative games. When the cooperative game is over, you often hear, "We *won*" (with emphasis on the "won"); in a competitive game you often hear, "*We* won, *we* won," in a taunting refrain (with the emphasis on the "we").

But children need a great deal of guidance and experience with cooperative games. Often games revised from competitive games revert to their competitive forms when the players are not familiar enough with the cooperative forms. Fortunately, a teacher or leader is more sought after to play cooperative games than competitive games. Apparently such a person is regarded as an asset to the whole group rather than as an obstacle or threat.

Active games with some pattern of motion seem to be especially enjoyable. Witnessing persons choosing to play cooperative games during times when a wide range of activities were at their disposal seems to substantiate the observation that cooperative games are both interesting and challenging to many players.

While you can tell just by looking that players enjoy cooperative games, there is a lack of controlled research evidence to indicate what might be the effects of cooperative games on different kinds of players. Cornelius and Lentz have described their own observations of the behavior of specific kinds of children engaged in cooperative play. They tell, for example, of a child who had frequent temper tantrums. When Arthur lost at a competitive game he would have outbursts of anger, striking out at anything and everything in his way. Although he found it difficult to wait while other players had their turn in a cooperative game and his behavior frequently caused the group to fail in its objective, he nevertheless was not as upset with losing in this setup and did not manifest the same frustration and rage. Perhaps not having been vanquished by another person, and sharing the loss with everyone playing, kept him at a more even emotional keel.

Of special interest are their observations of the cooperative game experiences of a mentally retarded child. Doris had trouble understanding the rules of the game. When it was her turn, the other members of the group, intent on having her contribute to their progress, carefully coached her in the steps to follow. When Doris performed successfully it was hard to judge whose joy and satisfaction were greater—hers for having mastered the skill, or the group's for having made her understand and be able to achieve success.

The subjective evidence and observational data point to the beneficial effects of cooperative activities on the personal and social growth of children. It remains, of course, for experimental data to validate this. In a society which believes in competition as a prime motivating force, it would be extremely interesting to investigate the effects on achievement as well as on personality when cooperation replaces competition as a motivating factor.

6 STAGE TWO: ESTABLISHING NORMS GOAL FOUR: DECISION-MAKING THROUGH CONSENSUS

The ground rules that determine how decisions are made in any particular classroom crucially affect the work of that group. In some classrooms a single member has enough power to railroad decisions through by coercion or by cajoling or influencing others. Other classes are run by majority rule, and still others—though these are rare—strive to come to unanimous agreement on decisions.

Decision-making by one powerful individual has its advantages. Decisions can be made quickly and smoothly; consequently, this is a very "efficient" method. Sometimes when the members of the class do not wish to take responsibility for themselves, they are all too happy to let one or two powerful or popular individuals make all the decisions. But such a method of decision-making has its disadvantages, too. For one, the one or two members of the class who are making the decision may not have all the information they would need to decide wisely. Other members might have special knowledge or expertise that is not tapped if only one or two people make the decisions. Furthermore, if all members haven't been consulted, they are not likely to be very committed to whatever decisions are made. Even though they may have indicated initially that they are willing for the individual(s) to make all the decisions, the other members may later attack or sabotage those decisions, or they may show a lack of enthusiasm in carrying them out.

Voting on issues and making decisions by majority rule has the advantage of encouraging more group members to share their information and opinions. This may result in decisions which are superior to those made by only a few individuals. More importantly, if more than half the students have voted for a decision, they will probably support the decision after it's made.

But voting also has its disadvantages. When an issue is decided simply by polling the members and letting the majority win, the group tends to become polarized. The object of discussion under these circumstances usually is to "win" the the upcoming vote rather than to arrive at the best decision. Consequently, members devote themselves to arguing vociferously for their point of view, seeking others who will support their position, and antagonizing those who do not agree with them. In this kind of voting situation, there are necessarily winners (the majority) and losers (the minority), and since a majority can be as few as one-half of the class plus one, the number of losers may be quite sizeable. Losers don't readily support decisions forced on them by the majority. They often feel alienated and bitter, and many times they look for opportunities to sabotage the decision that was made with which they disagreed. If they don't cooperate to achieve the group's goal or help to implement the decision, a lot of energy that could have been used to further the group's purposes is wasted. Thus majority rule can sometimes have negative effects on the work of the group.

But decision-making in classrooms does not have to be controlled by a few powerful individuals or by the vote of a majority. An alternative is consensus. In this approach to decision-making, members strive to arrive at a solution that *all* can agree to and support. In consensus, then, there are no losers. The ideas, expertise, and needs of all members are taken into serious consideration by the entire group. The group members work together to find the best solution for all, rather than combatting one another to prove that a particular point of view is "right." In attempting to reach consensus, everyone is required to listen carefully to all viewpoints instead of ignoring minority opinions. Hence, the group may avoid making serious mistakes, for they have access to information that the majority might otherwise overlook.

The search for a decision that all members can live with usually results in the entire group's being committed to the decision. Thus, no alienated minority remains to sabotage the work of the group. Once the group becomes even moderately skilled in the consensus approach, aggression, discourtesy, and hostility drop to much lower levels than in majority rule with its struggle to "win."

Many teachers have found that requiring a discussion group to seek consensus makes a dramatic difference in the members' interaction, even if they never actually achieve full consensus. Too often we give a group a topic to discuss—for example, "Why did the British lose the American Revolutionary War?"—and they rush through it, hitting only the high spots and more obvious points, never really grappling with the issues the way we would like them to. Student superficiality in dealing with discussion questions often causes teachers to reject group-centered discussion and revert to teacher-led discussion in order to assure that students have explored the topic deeply. Requiring the group to come to consensus on an answer, even if we admit that there is no one "right" answer to a question such as this, generally forces the students to consider the issues more deeply, to analyze their information more thoroughly, to listen to one another's opinions more closely and thoughtfully.

Despite its advantages, consensus-seeking cannot work and should not be attempted in every situation. Obviously, there are some topics the group may discuss that do not require members to come to any decision at all—open-ended sharing of values, experiences, and opinions, for example. To try to arrive at consensus on an issue such as "Is it more important to be honest or well liked?" would be ludicrous; because the very purpose of the question is to get students to share their diverse values, not to arrive at a group value. Even in some cases where a group decision is necessary, consensus is often time-consuming and may not be worth the effort. For example, a class is choosing which place to go on a field trip. The request for the bus must be submitted that day. If the vast majority of the students are in favor of one option, in this case the decision might best be based on a majority vote. Another case would be deciding whether to work a set of problems in class individually or in small groups. Polling the students and letting the majority rule is probably wiser than agonizing for hours until consensus is reached.

There is a point of diminishing returns that can be reached in any learning activity, and if there is likely to be little payoff (a better decision or improved skills of interaction) from a group's continuing to struggle toward consensus, the teacher may be wise in suggesting that the group abide by a majority vote. Nevertheless, it is important to establish as a norm for group interaction that consensus should be the *goal* of the group decision-making process.

HELPFUL TEACHER BEHAVIOR FOR ESTABLISHING NORM #4: DECISION-MAKING THROUGH CONSENSUS

Frame assignments for group-centered learning activities in a form that encourages the group to strive toward consensus.

In discussions about classroom procedures, or when a solution to a curricular problem is sought, encourage students to arrive at an answer that all members of the group can agree with, or support, or at least live with until it is proven satisfactory or unsatisfactory. For example, suppose you would like your class to consider a hypothetical situation in which a family has to decide whether to withdraw life-prolonging medical procedures from a hopelessly ill family member. Do not simply say, "Decide in your small groups what the family members should tell the doctor." Instead, it would be better to say, "Come to agreement as a group on what decision the family should make. Attempt to arrive at a decision that all members of your group can support." This will continually remind the group members that you expect them to consider thoughtfully the points of view of all members, not just the noisy few or even the majority.

When the group arrives at a decision, check whether consensus was reached.

Often in watching students as they work on a task, you can spot some who have dissented as the decision was made. When the group submits the decision, ask the persons who previously dissented whether they now support the group's decision. If they do not, the group obviously did not reach consensus and you can try to find out why. Early in the life of the group, you will have to find out if all members, including those with dissenting opinions, were listened to, if quieter members were encouraged to voice their opinions, and if the group checked to see where every person stood on the issue before making a final decision. With a group that is more mature, members probably did strive for consensus, and your role at this time becomes one of helping analyze what obstacles interfered with consensus and how to overcome them.

Do not force the class to reach an artificial consensus.

Sometimes in an effort to please you, all members will pretend to agree whether they do or not. Do not imply that the group has failed if consensus is not reached. The object of working for consensus is not really to make everyone agree, but to make students aware of the range of opinions in the group and to have them consider all those opinions thoughtfully.

If, after working for consensus for a reasonable length of time, the group discovers that major differences in values or opinions exist, have the members present you with a majority opinion and a minority opinion, with each faction stating the reasons for its position. This approach is, of course, the one used by the U.S. Supreme Court, where decisions are made by majority rule, but the minority may write a dissenting opinion which is given equally widespread publicity and which, like the majority opinion, may be quoted in future court rulings.

Help the class understand that consensus can be achieved in many ways.

Explore with the group members these different ways consensus is achieved:

1. One side persuades the other. This, of course, is what most groups think they are doing when they simply vote with majority rule, but they overlook the fact that they might not at all have convinced everyone in the group. When consensus is achieved through persuasion, it means that virtually all in the group agree that the arguments in favor of one point of view are compelling and overwhelming, and they forsake their previous positions and support that point of view.

2. One side gives in. Often a group of persons will believe that it is not worth the energy to defend the position they have been supporting and they decide to abandon their position. This approach to consensus is not a healthy one, however, if the group capitulates just to avoid a fuss or because they're outnumbered, and they do not really support the other position. The point of view of dissenters is essential to creative decision-making; often a single person holds key information that can save the group from an error (such as may occur in playing the *Mystery Games* described earlier). The conflict that results from differing opinions should be viewed by the group as valuable, and giving in should be discouraged unless it is based on thought and conviction.

Students need to learn when to give in and when to continue to fight for their stand. People should be able to change their minds freely as new information becomes available. When working for consensus, people should be free to explore a number of positions and should not feel they are deserting their party if they change their minds, or simply decide that an issue is not important to them and that they are willing to let others make the decision, or that others know more about this particular decision than they do. Sometimes people may decide that the inconvenience to them of accepting a viewpoint other than their own is minor compared to the major inconvenience that their position would cause others. On the other hand, individuals should be free to refuse to relinquish their positions if an issue is important to them.

So, working for consensus not only forces individuals to evaluate their own and others' positions, but also forces them to look at how important their position is to them. Sometimes it may be the majority who decide to change. For example, if the class is trying to reach consensus on a day for the class picnic, the minority who prefer Saturday over Sunday may decide simply to give in. However, if one student cannot come on Sunday because of strong religious convictions, the whole class may decide that their convenience is less important than this student's values and change the picnic to Saturday.

3. Both sides find a new alternative. Disagreement can sometimes be overcome if the two sides stop trying to defend the positions they've taken and attempt to find a different solution that will satisfy both groups. Frequently neither group has to give up anything, and both groups come out feeling that they've "won."

4.   The group redefines the issue.   Sincere search for consensus frequently leads participants to realize that their conflict is caused by semantic difficulties or by a misperception of the other party's position. Sometimes both sides realize that they have overstated their positions and, as they strive for consensus, they moderate their stands and find a way of viewing the issue that both can support.

5.   Each side gives in a little.   Sometimes a decision or course of action can be agreed on that meets most of the needs of both sides rather than all the needs of one side and none of the other's. Persons accustomed to using the consensus model of decision-making realize that to give up a little of what one side wants is a small sacrifice to make in order to gain the satisfaction and support of the other members of the group.

6.   Both sides agree to let it ride.   Sometimes all involved agree that they do not yet have enough information to make a prudent decision, or that they are too upset to arrive at a workable solution. They may choose to table the issue until they can return with the knowledge and attitudes required to make a rational decision.

However, they should make sure that they are not letting it ride as an excuse for avoiding conflict and escaping from the bother of serious negotiation. We have all sat through faculty meetings in which, whenever an issue arose that sparked controversy and disagreement someone quickly made a motion to table the issue "for further study." For many people, disagreement and conflict are signs that something is going wrong in the group, and their impulse is to retreat to something more pleasant. On the contrary, conflict is usually an indication that everyone in the group feels free to express an opinion, that a diversity of ideas is being generated, and that the issue is significant to the group. Viewed in this light, conflict can be regarded as a prelude to decision-making of higher quality than would result if everyone quickly agreed. Members of the group must watch closely to determine whether they are deciding to let it ride simply to avoid confronting disagreement, or whether there are legitimate reasons to postpone a decision.

Offer suggestions for how members can be helpful to a group that is trying to achieve consensus.

Jay Hall[1] offers the following guidelines, which you can summarize for students:

(1) Avoid arguing for your own position. Present it as lucidly and logically as possible, but be sensitive to, and consider seriously, the reactions of the group in any subsequent presentation of the same point.

(2) Avoid "win-lose" stalemates in the discussion of opinions. Discard the notion that someone must win and someone must lose in the discussion; when impasses occur, look for the next most acceptable alternative for all the parties involved.

(3) Avoid changing your mind only in order to avoid conflict and to reach agreement and harmony. Withstand pressures to yield which have no objective or logically sound foundation. Strive for enlightened flexibility, but avoid outright capitulation.

---

[1]Hall, Jay. *Toward Group Effectiveness*. Conroe, Texas: Teleometrics International, 1971, page 8. Used with permission.

(4) Avoid conflict-reducing techniques such as the majority vote, averaging, bargaining, coin-flipping, trading out, and the like. Treat differences of opinion as indicative of an incomplete sharing of relevant information on someone's part, either about task issues, emotional data, or "gut level" intuitions.

(5) View differences of opinion as both natural and helpful rather than as a hindrance in decision-making. Generally, the more ideas expressed, the greater the likelihood of conflict, but the richer the array of resources as well.

(6) View initial agreement as suspect. Explore the reasons underlying apparent agreement; make sure people have arrived at the same conclusions for either the same basic reasons or for complementary reasons.

(7) Avoid subtle forms of influence and decision modification; e.g., when a dissenting member finally agrees, don't feel that he must be "rewarded" by having his own way on some subsequent point.

Model consensus-seeking behavior at all times when working with the class.

Any time you ask the class for opinions—for example, whether members think the unit test should be on Wednesday or on Thursday—do not stop after the first couple of opinions have been volunteered. Don't be taken in by the "handclasp" approach, in which one powerful or popular or especially vocal student expresses an opinion which is immediately seconded by a crony. These two opinions, even if no opposing ones are expressed, do not constitute consensus. Poll the entire class with some voting procedure—show of hands, secret ballot, voice vote—to assess where the entire group stands.

Watch particularly for students who do not vote and ask them why. Note which students hold minority opinions and make sure you ask them to explain their opinions, rather than simply saying, "Well, it looks like most of you want the test on Wednesday, so Wednesday it is." It could be that one of the dissenting students knows about some social event planned for Tuesday night that no one else has heard about yet. That single, quiet student could save the group from making a decision most members would later regret. In your own work with students, treat dissenting opinions with the respect you expect them to show one another when they work as a group.

STRUCTURED EXPERIENCES FOR ESTABLISH-ING NORM #4: DECISION-MAKING THROUGH CONSENSUS

1. Twelve Angry Men.

Students may question the value of struggling through the often frustrating process of attempting to achieve consensus. "Why not just take a vote and let the majority rule?" they may ask. One way to have them arrive at their own answer is to have them read the play *Twelve Angry Men* or arrange for them to view the film version.[2] In this play a jury is deliberating the guilt of a suspected murderer. A majority of 11 persons votes for conviction immediately and is ready to go home. But

---

[2]*Twelve Angry Men* by Reginald Rose, available in *Great Television Plays*, edited by William I. Kaufman (New York: Dell Publishing Company, 1969). Film distributed by United Artists "16," 729 Seventh Avenue, New York, New York 10019. An interesting activity utilizing the film version of *Twelve Angry Men*, the "Twelve Angry Men Prediction Task," can be found on pages 13-16 of *The 1972 Annual Handbook for Group Facilitators* by John E. Jones and J. William Pfeiffer (LaJolla: University Associates, 1972).

a lone juror has made a number of careful observations and, because of his background, has information that the others do not possess. Since a jury must reach consensus to convict a person of murder, the other 11 are forced to listen to his arguments and finally are persuaded by them, thus saving an innocent man's life.

2.   Surviving in the Rockies.[3]

This activity not only deals with the question, "Why not just take a vote and let the majority rule?" but also demonstrates that improved performance results when people work together instead of individually. The activity requires students first to complete a task, on their own; then to work with a group voting by majority rule; and finally to work with the same group utilizing consensus. Since the problem has a verifiable answer, it is possible to use quantitative measures to compare the results obtained in each of the three situations.

To prepare for the activity, duplicate at least three copies of the worksheet below for each member of the class. A total of about two hours (perhaps on successive days) will be needed to complete all three steps.

Surviving in the Rockies

Imagine that a friend stops by your house on a Saturday morning in October and suggests that you go with him for a day-long drive in the mountains to

---

[3]Adapted from pp. 117-120 of *Human Interaction in Education* by Gene Stanford and Albert E. Roark (Allyn & Bacon, 1974) and used here with permission of the publisher. It is based on the well-known NASA "Lost on the Moon" exercise devised by Jay Hall of Teleometrics International. Materials for the NASA exercise, which makes an excellent alternative to or follow-up exercise for "Surviving in the Rockies," can be obtained from Teleometrics International (P.O. Drawer 1850, Conroe, Texas 77301) or can be found in Pfeiffer and Jones' Vol. I of *A Handbook of Structured Experiences for Human Relations Training*.

try out his new Jeep. You quickly pull on jeans, a sweatshirt, and sneakers to go along. By late afternoon you are on a trail in a remote part of the Rockies, when suddenly a snowstorm blows up. The trail soon becomes almost impassable and you can hardly see where you are going. Suddenly the Jeep starts to skid and you plunge several hundred feet down a steep mountainside. Your friend is killed instantly and the Jeep is completely wrecked, but fortunately you have only a few scratches. By your best estimate you are 30 to 40 miles from the nearest source of help. Luckily you discover a summer cabin nearby. Although it has no heat except a wood-burning fireplace and no telephone, it does offer shelter and about a week's supply of food. You soon realize that you cannot hope to stay in the cabin until you are rescued, for no one has any idea where to start looking for you. Therefore, when the storm starts to abate, leaving almost three feet of dry powder snow, you decide to try to follow the trail back to civilization. You are fortunate that the cabin is well stocked with camping equipment and other supplies and you can take almost anything you want, but you know that your survival over the three days it will probably take you to reach help will depend partly on how carefully you select what equipment to take. Below is a list of some of the materials the cabin contains and their weight. Decide which of the following items you will wear or carry, not exceeding a total of 50 pounds.

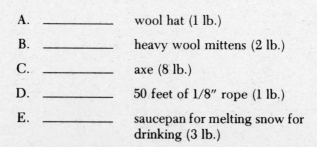

A. _____ wool hat (1 lb.)

B. _____ heavy wool mittens (2 lb.)

C. _____ axe (8 lb.)

D. _____ 50 feet of 1/8″ rope (1 lb.)

E. _____ saucepan for melting snow for drinking (3 lb.)

F. _____   folding camping saw (1 lb.)

G. _____   rock-climbing gear, including rock hammer, pitons, etc. (10 lb.)

H. _____   150 feet of 7/16″ rope (8 lb.)

I. _____   gasoline camp stove and fuel (10 lb.)

J. _____   plastic canteen filled with water (2 lb.)

K. _____   one large can of beef stew (10 lb.)

L. _____   fire-starting kit, including matches (1/2 lb.)

M. _____   heavy wool jacket with hood (10 lb.)

N. _____   pack frame and bag (6 lb.)

O. _____   five two-pound cans of soup and vegetables (10 lb.)

P. _____   sleeping bag (5 lb.)

Q. _____   downhill skis, bindings, poles (10 lb.)

R. _____   air mattress (3 lb.)

S. _____   down-filled jacket without hood (3 lb.)

T. _____   high-top hunting boots (6 lb.)

U. _____   snowshoes (5 lb.)

V. _____   canvas tent (15 lb.)

W. _____   plastic tarp (2 lb.)

X. _____   eight boxes of high protein dry cereal (4 lb. total)

Y. _____ first-aid kit with splints and other equipment for setting bones (4 lb.)

Z. _____ first-aid kit without splints, etc. (1 lb.)

AA. _____ heavy wool pants (4 lb.)

BB. _____ knife with can opener (1/2 lb.)

For the first step of this activity give students the worksheet and have them mark their answers following the instructions on the sheet. Emphasize that each student is to work entirely alone, without consulting other students or any other resources. To save time, you might wish to assign this step as homework, but emphasize that everyone must bring the worksheet back to class and that students are not to consult with anyone when making their individual choices. Have students put their names on the individual worksheets and turn them in to you for scoring. Do not let students score their own papers and do not tell them the correct answers.

After all students have turned in the first worksheet, give them each a fresh copy of the worksheet and have them form into small groups of five to seven (or meet as a total class). Instruct the students to do the task again, but this time to choose the items by majority vote of their group. Suggest that they vote after a minimum of discussion, and point out that their answers this time may be different from their independent answers.

While they are working as a group, score their individual worksheets. The correct answers (on page 197) were supplied by Bill May, author of *Mountain Search and Rescue,* and a member of the Rocky Mountain Rescue Group; and by Bob Bruce, merchandise manager of Holubar Mountaineering, Ltd., and a member of the certification committee of the United States Ski Association.

Answers for Surviving in the Rockies:

A.	1 lb.	R.	3 lbs.
B.	2 lbs.	S.	3 lbs.
D.	1 lb.	T.	6 lbs.
E.	1 lb.	U.	5 lbs.
F.	1 lb.	W.	2 lbs.
J.	2 lbs.	X.	4. lbs.
L.	1/2 lb.	Z.	1 lb.
N.	6 lbs.	AA.	4 lbs.
P.	5 lbs.	BB.	1/2 lb.

To score the individual answer sheets, count one point for each item that is on the student's list but is not on the answer key. Also count one point for each item that is on the answer key but not on the student's list. Total these points to get the individual's overall score. (The lower the score, the more accurate the student's answer.)

Arrange the individual worksheets in groups to correspond with the groups the students are working in. Locate the answer sheet of the individual in each group who has the best (lowest) score.

After the groups have finished voting, ask each group to record their choices on one answer sheet. Assign each group a number and have them write this number on their answer sheet. Collect the answer sheets.

Then give each student a third copy of the problem sheet. Instruct them to remain in their same groups and do the exercise again, but this time they are to come to agreement (consensus) on which items to take. Include the following explanation in your instructions: "In trying to arrive at your answers, be sure to use reasoning and factual information. You should neither refuse to compromise nor should you give in just to make things easier. Try hard to understand the suggestions of other members, even when they disagree with your own choices. But don't change your mind if you are not convinced just in order to avoid conflict: make sure you can support any decision the group comes to. Do not use majority rule to decide on an answer; strive for complete agreement by all members of the group." Have each group record their choices on an answer sheet.

While the groups are trying to arrive at consensus, score the group answer sheets showing the choices made by majority vote, following the same procedure as described above for the individual answers. Prepare a summary chart that will show: (1) the individual score of each group's most accurate individual, (2) the score resulting from majority rule, and (3) the score resulting from decision by consensus.

After the groups have arrived at consensus, or have come as close to consensus as possible in the available time, collect and score their answer sheets. Tell the students the correct answers according to the experts. Then complete the chart and show it to the students.

Group No.	Best Individual Score	Voting Score	Consensus Score
1			
2			
3			
4			

Give students their own individual scores and tell them to compare these with the other scores on the chart. Suggest they ask themselves questions such as the following:

Was my individual score better (i.e., lower) or worse than the score my group achieved? (If worse, then this would indicate that working with a group results in answers that are more informed or accurate.)

Was the score of the best individual in my group better (i.e., lower) or worse than the scores arrived at by group voting and consensus? (If the best individual's score was better, the group obviously ignored an "expert" in their midst; if the group's scores were better, the group situation produced more accurate results than even the best individual could do alone—the synergistic effect.)

Did my group do better (i.e., score lower) when voting or when striving for consensus?

Continue with a class discussion of questions such as:

How can the differences in scores be explained?

Why was consensus harder than voting?

What problems did you have in coming to consensus?

What ways of working together did you develop while trying to come to consensus?

Which method of decision-making (individual, group with majority vote, consensus) made you *feel* best about the decision?

3.   Other Consensus Tasks.

A number of other consensus exercises, similar in format to *Surviving in the Rockies* described above, can be found in *A Handbook of Structured Experiences for Human Relations Training*.[4] The following exercises are thought to be particularly useful:

---

[4]Pfeiffer, J. William, John E. Jones, *A Handbook of Structured Experiences for Human Relations Training*, 5 vols., La Jolla, Ca., 1973-75

Occupational Prestige Ranking Task, Vol. II, pp. 22-24.

Kerner Report Ranking Task, Vol. III, pp. 71-77.

Supervisory Behavior and *Aims of Education* Ranking Tasks, Vol. III, pp. 93-96.

A Collection of Consensus Tasks: *Life Crises, Dating Preferences, Trustworthiness of Occupations, Values of Young People, Whom to Leave Behind, Being a Teenager, Community Leader, Characteristics of a Good Teacher,* Vol. IV, pp. 51-65.

Arriving at consensus is sometimes difficult and time-consuming, and may frequently prove frustrating to those who prefer quick and effortless decisions. Consensus demands considerable patience on the part of participants, and at least minimal competence in the skills of group interaction, especially in listening carefully and encouraging others to contribute. Participants' attitudes must change from the "win/lose" orientation to one of "how can we assure that everyone will win?" Thus, the skills and attitudes of cooperation previously described are important prerequisites for the use of consensus. Since consensus requires a high level of skill and considerable experience, miracles are not going to occur overnight. Nevertheless, with guidance and experience, in time a group may achieve consensus as a goal of interaction.

7 STAGE TWO: ESTABLISHING NORMS GOAL FIVE: CONFRONTING PROBLEMS

"Not everything that is faced can be changed," wrote James Baldwin, "but nothing can be changed until it is faced." Never is this more true than when groups encounter problems. Unless members are willing to confront and learn from their problems, there is little hope that the group can improve its functioning. When members ignore a problem—whether it be the unwillingness of some persons to contribute, or a tendency for the group to stray off the topic, or lack of commitment to the task, or hostility between some members or leaders who dominate the group—the problem doesn't go away. It continues to plague the group, and often actually becomes more acute because it's been allowed to fester.

Most of us have the impulse to avoid confronting interpersonal problems because we're uncomfortable handling the tensions that confrontation might produce. Teachers usually find it easier to intervene unilaterally and to deal with a problem by scolding, nagging, joking, or altering the situation, rather than sitting down with the group that is having a problem to discuss it. Students are no more enthusiastic about confronting problems than are teachers. They'd prefer to complain in private, or protest to the teacher individually, or give up in disgust. Talking directly with those involved about what goes on in our relationships is a new and difficult experience.

But only by overcoming the impulse to avoid confrontation can a group hope to develop into maturity. As an example, let me describe an episode with my high school English class which was my first venture into helping a group confront a problem instead of intervening to cover up the problem. It all started when Linda came to me and asked to be transferred to another class. She was a rather unattractive girl, overweight, with stringy hair and bad acne. She tried hard to take an active part in the class and to be friendly to the other students. The acknowledged leader of the class was Bob, popular throughout the school for his personal charm and for his accomplishments on the track team. Linda annoyed Bob. He made sarcastic comments to her in hopes of shutting her up when she contributed to class discussions. Linda was eager for Bob's approval and resented his cutting remarks, but didn't know what to do.

The problem between Bob and Linda directly affected the entire class. A number of students had sided with Linda, encouraging her privately to do something to stop Bob's cruel treatment. Bob's friends defended him strongly against charges that he was mistreating Linda.

Realizing that moving Linda to a different class would only be "sweeping it under the rug," I decided that I must help the entire group to confront the problem. I wasn't too sure I knew how, but I decided to try. Rather than counseling Bob and Linda separately in hopes of working something out, I asked their cooperation in presenting the problem to the entire class. I began by telling the group that I had perceived that there was a problem between Bob and Linda and I wondered if they had noticed it also. I asked each person in the class to tell

what was happening. I told them I didn't want their judg-
ments, but rather their objective descriptions of what they saw
happening.

After the students had shared their perceptions, I asked
Linda to state specifically what she resented about Bob's
behavior in class, and then I had Bob tell what he resented
about Linda's behavior. Although they were a bit nervous
about doing so, both described honestly how they felt. Linda
said that she didn't like the way Bob seemed to be making fun
of her in class. "It embarrasses me and I feel like crawling
under the desk. You sound like you're just joking, but you're
putting me down." Bob stated that he resented Linda's talking
so much in class discussions, "even when you don't know a
thing about the topic."

Then I asked Linda to tell Bob exactly what she would
like him to do in order to make her more comfortable in the
class, and Bob did the same with her. Linda said she wished
Bob would quit making fun of her. "Just don't speak to me at
all if you can't help cutting me down." Bob wanted her to use
better judgment in deciding when to contribute to discussions.
"Don't talk for the sake of talking. Wait until you really have
something to say." They each agreed to work at meeting the
other's demands, and thus with the help of the other students a
solution was worked out that would let each save face and
assure the future comfort of both.

Finally, in order to demonstrate to the two members
that they were important to and accepted by the group, I had
each member of the class state one thing he or she liked or
appreciated about Linda and about Bob. This renewed the
group's cohesiveness and signaled the end of the polarization
between the students.[1]

---

[1] This procedure is similar to the "3R Strategy" (see page 244) and to the
"R-D-A" approach described in *Values Clarification*, by Sidney B. Simon,
Leland W. Howe, and Howard Kirschenbaum, Hart Publishing Co., New
York, 1972.

This experience taught me that helping a group confront its problems openly is not nearly as scary as I had imagined. And the outcome was so overwhelmingly positive that I was convinced it was worth the effort. By taking the 20 minutes to talk, the group was relieved of a problem that was distracting members and sapping emotional energy. They could then turn their attention to their work.

Confronting interpersonal problems openly is essential if a group is to develop its maximum effectiveness. But it also has an additional benefit. Students develop skills that will be useful in countless interpersonal situations in the future. Instead of feeling helpless when things are not going well in a group, these students will know how to examine the problems and work out satisfactory solutions. They will not be dependent on a teacher or group leader to take responsibility for making things right.

HELPFUL TEACHER BEHAVIOR FOR ESTABLISHING NORM #5: CONFRONTING PROBLEMS

Observe the group and describe its problem behavior.

Initially, the teacher's role in helping a group confront its problems openly is that of the observer giving feedback. The teacher brings problems to the group's attention and facilitates the process of analyzing and solving them. In some cases, as with Bob and Linda, you may have to bring out into the open something that the group is already aware of, and encourage members to talk about it openly rather than covertly. In other cases, the group may not be aware of what is causing problems. By presenting your observations to the group, you can help focus attention on what is happening.

When presenting your observations about its problems to the group, you might keep these points in mind:

(1) Invite group members to describe their problem behavior before you give them your perceptions of it. If they can identify their own problems, they'll be more likely to deal with them honestly than if you tell them about their problems. For example, rather than saying "This discussion was not successful because you didn't stay on the topic," ask "How well were you able to meet your goal?"

(2) Describe specific behavior rather than talking abstractly. For example, "Bill, you and Ted sat apart from the group and spoke only when someone else asked you a question" is more helpful than "Bill, you and Ted weren't involved."

(3) Check the accuracy of your perceptions by asking whether the group members see their behavior as you did.

(4) Avoid words that imply a judgment. Let the group evaluate whether the behavior you have observed is good (i.e., helpful in reaching the goal) or not. Don't say "Today's discussion was not what I would have expected of you ninth graders. You were really acting immature." A better approach would be "Throughout today's discussion many of you interrupted the speaker. What effect do you think this had on the discussion?"

(5) Try to focus on behavior that the group can do something about, not on factors beyond its control. It's not helpful to tell average students who may be doing their best "You certainly didn't demonstrate much insight into this issue," or to chide students for being overly preoccupied with an event that's about to take place (a visit to the school by Joe Namath, for example). Ask yourself "Is this something I can logically and reasonably expect this group to be able to correct or

change?" If the answer is no, don't burden them with it.

(6) Ask members of the group to repeat, paraphrase, or summarize the behavior you described in order to determine whether you have communicated clearly.

Let the group monitor its own process.

After a group has had sufficient experience with the teacher describing their problem behavior, members should be encouraged to monitor their own group process. That is, they should observe what helps or interferes with their group work. Soon the group should be able to identify problems when they occur and discuss them openly. Sometimes members may wish to use one of the structured experiences suggested later in this chapter—such as having one member serve as process observer, or filling out questionnaires and examining the results. At other times they may simply wish to talk over what is happening in the group that is impeding progress.

Help students distinguish descriptive feedback from brutal honesty.

When they are urged to talk openly about problems in the group, some students mistakenly believe they should say whatever is on their minds, regardless of the consequences. This attitude is perhaps based on the misconception that "honesty" is the highest value in group interaction, even if it results in members being cruel to one another. It is not possible to preclude completely the possibility of students hurting the feelings of others when talking openly about problems in the group, but you can minimize the chance of students confronting one another in a harmful way. Present the following guidelines to the class and require they be used when members discuss one another's behavior in the group:

(1) Urge the person involved to talk about the problem behavior before you describe it.

(2) Describe only *behavior*. Tell how the behavior looks, sounds, and feels to you. Do not interpret the behavior or motives of the person. For example, it is better to say "You interrupt other people when they're talking" (description of behavior), than "You don't care about other people in the group" (inference about motives).

(3) Don't judge other people's behavior; simply describe it and explain how that behavior is keeping the group from achieving its goal. It's better to say "We could finish the job faster if you would share your ideas with us," than "It's not right for you to just sit there and not participate."

(4) Try to avoid general words like "hostile," "uncooperative," "selfish," "domineering," etc. Instead describe the *behavior* that leads you to infer these characteristics: "You speak in a gruff tone of voice and frown a lot" or "You work out the problems by yourself and usually finish before everyone else, but you don't offer to help the rest of us understand how to do them" or "You take all the best materials for yourself and won't share them, even when we ask politely" or "You tell everyone what to do and don't give anyone else a chance to make suggestions."

(5) Don't focus on behavior that the person has no control over, such as a speech impediment or being slow to understand.

(6) Be specific about what you think the person could do to be more helpful to the group. Make specific

suggestions for behavior changes, even if you're not sure the person will accept them.

(7) Ask the person to whom you're talking to summarize what you've said in order to check how clearly you've communicated.

(8) Ask other members of the group whether they see things the way you do. You may be misperceiving the situation.

Monitor discussions carefully to make sure that the guidelines are followed. Whenever members violate any of the guidelines, intervene to reestablish the desired procedure. For example, if Jerry starts yelling at Kevin "The reason we're not getting anywhere is because you're so darned pushy!" ask Jerry to explain what Kevin is doing that causes Jerry to think Kevin is "pushy."

Help students distinguish confronting problems from "tattling."

Many students become uncomfortable when asked to talk over the way they are working together, for they equate it with "telling on" one another. For example, when I asked Mark to tell who hadn't participated in a discussion, he wasn't too happy about it. Here's how he descibed the episode in his journal:

> For the second time Mr. Stanford has called on me to point out who didn't participate in the discussion. I do not like to do that because I do not like to "accuse" or give anybody a bad name by pointing at him for sitting like a log during the discussion. I did feel a little uneasy when I was saying the names, but I guess someone had to say it.

I had apparently failed to help the class understand that

describing the behavior of others is valuable and healthy because it helps the group improve its functioning. They still were viewing it as reporting one another to the teacher. The persons named felt unfairly "accused," and Mark was uneasy because he thought that he would be rejected by the group as a "tattler." Before I asked this question I should have made sure the students understood that the purpose is to help the group improve its work and ultimately make everyone feel more comfortable together, not simply to identify and punish offenders.

Respect your own limits.

Although as a general rule interpersonal problems that are hindering the group's progress are best examined openly, there are times when the teacher may feel that an issue should be left alone. Helping a group confront problems is a little scary for most of us, particularly until we've become accustomed to it. You may rightly feel that some problems are simply too explosive or potentially upsetting to be brought into the open. You should do in this regard whatever you are comfortable with. Not every problem has to be confronted, and if you aren't comfortable opening up certain issues, you can begin with less threatening problems. Insofar as you can, help the group examine openly the problems it is having rather than ignoring them.

STRUCTURED EXPERIENCES FOR CONFRONTING PROBLEMS

The process of confronting problems has two aspects— seeing the problem and solving the problem. Often a group isn't aware of the existence of a problem, and thus a feedback procedure is frequently required to show members what is happening. At first, the teacher takes the initiative in providing the group with feedback about its performance. Eventually the group should learn to work out procedures for monitoring progress and examining problems. Once the group learns to identify problems, structured procedures for seeking solutions can be helpful.

Seeing the Problem

Since talking openly about interpersonal relations is likely to make a group somewhat uncomfortable at first, it is best to start with procedures that are minimally threatening and move gradually toward more open discussion. In general, anonymous data is less threatening than reports from observers, and both of these procedures are less threatening than asking the group members to talk directly to one another about the group's problems.

1. Questionnaires.

Administer a questionnaire to the members of the group to gather data about possible problems the group is experiencing. Use one of the forms provided here or make up your own with questions particularly suited to your group. You may wish to choose a few of the items presented here instead of using the whole questionnaire. Tell students *not* to put their names on the questionnaires, so that the results are completely anonymous. Compile the results and summarize them orally to the class, or post the summary in the classroom for students to look over at leisure, or distribute a copy of the summary to each member. Ask the group to discuss what conclusions they can draw from the data, posing questions such as the following:

> What can we learn about the way the group is functioning by looking at these results?

> What things about the group seem to need improvement?

How might we go about making the needed changes?

Which of the approaches to change that have been suggested are we willing to commit ourselves to?

Group Process Questionnaire

INSTRUCTIONS: Write brief answers to each of the questions. Do not sign your name.

(1) Do you usually have a chance to talk as much as you want to in group activities in this class?

(2) Does something usually "bug" you during class activities? If so, what?

(3) Who does not seem to contribute toward the work of the group?

(4) What could the group do to make you more comfortable during class activities?

(5) Who seems to be doing most of the work of the group?

(6) What could the group do to improve the way members work together?

Group Climate Questionnaire

INSTRUCTIONS: Below is a series of statements, each beginning "With this group I. . . ." Use the five-point scale provided below to indicate how you feel about each statement. Put an X in the space that most closely represents your response.

R—RARELY means from 0 to 15 per cent of the time

S—SOMETIMES means from 16 to 35 per cent of the time

F—FREQUENTLY means from 36 to 65 per cent of the time

G—GENERALLY means from 66 to 85 per cent of the time

A—ALMOST ALWAYS means from 86 to 100 per cent of the time

Please report your immediate feelings rather than spending a great deal of time considering each item. There are no right or wrong answers. What is important is that you indicate honestly how you feel. Do *not* sign your name to this form.

WITH THIS GROUP I . . . :

(1) can express warm feelings

           R S F G A

(2) can express feelings of anger

           R S F G A

(3) shut out ideas different from mine

           R S F G A

(4) enjoy letting others know me

           R S F G A

(5) worry about my goofs

           R S F G A

(6) feel comfortable

           R S F G A

(7) recognize and can let others
know my feelings

__ __ __ __ __
R S F G A

(8) attempt to relate to only a
few members of the class

__ __ __ __ __
R S F G A

(9) put on a false front

__ __ __ __ __
R S F G A

(10) am unsure of myself

__ __ __ __ __
R S F G A

(11) am aware of others' feelings
about themselves

__ __ __ __ __
R S F G A

(12) am unaware of how others
see me

__ __ __ __ __
R S F G A

(13) feel that others ignore me

__ __ __ __ __
R S F G A

(14) feel that others care about
me

__ __ __ __ __
R S F G A

(15) feel that others do not listen
to me

__ __ __ __ __
R S F G A

(16) feel nervous

__ __ __ __ __
R S F G A

(17) feel that others tear me
down

__ __ __ __ __
R S F G A

(18) feel that others make fun of
me when I make mistakes

__ __ __ __ __
R S F G A

(19) feel that others like me

__ __ __ __ __
R S F G A

(20) feel that others do not see
me as I am

    R S F G A

(21) feel that others are cold

    R S F G A

(22) feel that others are insincere

    R S F G A

(23) feel that others are
trustworthy

    R S F G A

(24) feel that others are impatient

    R S F G A

Group Behavior Questionnaire[2]

INSTRUCTIONS: Answer all questions by naming members from the group. Base your answers on interaction that occurred in this class. Be sure to choose *two* people for each answer. You can use the same name more than once if you need to. Do not sign your name.

(1)   Which two members of the group can most easily influence others to change their opinions?

(2)   Which two are

[2]Reprinted from J. William Pfeiffer and John E. Jones (Eds.), *A Handbook of Structured Experiences for Human Relations Training*, Volume III (Rev.). La Jolla, Calif.: University Associates, 1974. Used with permission.

least able to influence others to change their opinions? _____ _____

(3) Which two have clashed most sharply during class discussions and other activities? _____ _____

(4) Which two are most highly accepted by the group as a whole? _____ _____

(5) Which two are most ready to protect and support members who are under attack? _____ _____

(6) Which two try to keep themselves in the limelight as much as possible? _____ _____

(7) Which two are most likely to put group goals above personal needs? _____ _____

(8) Which two are most likely to put personal needs above group goals? _____ _____

(9) Which two have been most ready to discuss topics not directly related to the task of the group? _____ _____

(10) Which two have shown the greatest desire to accomplish something? _____ _____

(11) Which two strive most to avoid conflict in the group discussions?   _____ _____

(12) Which two tend to withdraw from active discussion when strong differences begin to appear?   _____ _____

(13) Which two have sought to help in the resolution of differences that arise between others?   _____ _____

(14) Which two have wanted the group to be warm, friendly, and comfortable?   _____ _____

(15) Which two have competed the most with others?   _____ _____

(16) Which two have tried to do the most to keep the group on the ball?   _____ _____

(17) With which two would you choose to work on a project?   _____ _____

(18) To which two do you usually talk the least?   _____ _____

(19) To which two would you turn for help if you were in trouble?   _____ _____

(20) Which two in the group would you be

most likely to trust with
a secret?   _____ _____

(21)   Which two in the
group make you nervous
or ill at ease?   _____ _____

2. Observation.

Have one or two members of the group, chosen either
by you or by the group, sit outside the circle as the group works
and observe the interaction in the group. The observers can be
instructed to take notes on how the group could improve its
functioning, or they can be assigned to look for specific things,
such as the number of times students encourage others to talk,
or instances in which members do not listen to one another. Or,
provide the observers with a form such as one of those
suggested below on which to record their observations.

Questions for Observers

(1) Who is talking the most?

(2) Who is talking the least?

(3) What attempts do members make to encourage
     others to contribute?

(4) What attempts do members make to link their
     contributions to previous contributions?

(5) Do group members listen to one another? If not,
     jot down examples.

(6) How effectively is the group working toward its goal?

(7) What might members do to improve the way they are working together?

MEMBERSHIP ROLE OBSERVATION FORM

INSTRUCTIONS: List the names of the group members down the left-hand side of the form. Each time a member seems to be playing one of the positive or negative roles listed across the top, place a check mark in the appropriate square.

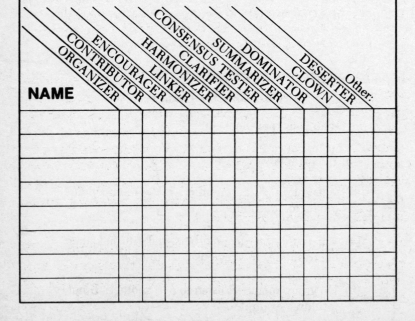

Who-Talks-To-Whom Observation Form

INSTRUCTIONS: Draw a circle (or other diagram) that represents the way the group is seated. Write the names of members to indicate their positions in the seating arrangement. As the group works together, draw an arrow from each speaker to the person addressed. If the member talks to the group as a whole, draw the arrow to the center of the circle.

When observers report back to the group, require them to adhere to the guidelines previously suggested for giving feedback on group behavior (see page 207). Other suggestions that may help the observers:

(1) Tell the group members what they are doing right as well as what they're doing wrong.

(2) Don't overwhelm the group with too many different pieces of information. Stick to the most important things you observed.

Another way to utilize observers is to divide the class into two groups, and have one group observe the other. Have the group members who will work sit in a circle, with the observers seated in a larger circle behind them. Assign each person in the outer circle to observe one member of the inner circle. Have observers take notes on the behavior of their partners in the inner circle. Afterwards, have the observers report their findings to their partners, adhering to the guidelines for giving feedback.

Finally, it is possible to allow the group to observe itself by recording a classroom activity on audio tape or video tape and playing it back. Ask members to identify the strengths and weaknesses of their work together.

3. Discussion.

Once the group has become accustomed to examining its own process, it is possible simply to ask members to talk about how they are doing. For example, when a particular problem is showing up in the interaction, or simply at random, you can have members consider questions such as:

> How are you working as a group?
>
> What problems are you having getting your task accomplished?
>
> How do you feel about what is happening in the group right now?
>
> Have you been listening carefully to one another?
>
> Are you building on one another's contributions?

After a brief discussion, members continue to work at their task, hopefully with improved results.

A discussion can also take place after the group has finished work (or a few minutes before the end of the class period). Have the students consider questions such as "How well did you achieve your goal as a group?" or "How could you have improved your work as a group?"

After a discussion of this type occurred in Janet's class, she wrote in her journal:

> *In class today we talked about who could influence us the most and also who seemed to listen to each of us the most. Bruce, Nancy, and Tom said that no one seems to listen to them. It could be the "way" they speak up. Bruce has really good ideas, but seems to say them at the wrong times or too softly. Nancy just talks too softly. She hardly ever says anything, but when she does I barely hear her and I'm one of the only ones who listens to everyone. I really don't have room to criticize, though. I usually don't say anything, though, unless I have something of value to say. I do*

> *use a forceful approach so they at least hear me,*
> *whether they agree or not. I try to make sure that all or*
> *most of the kids are paying attention.*

With groups that are well developed and highly cohesive, you might find the following procedure appropriate for helping students openly confront problems within the group. Seat the group in a circle. Have everybody look around and then write down the name of the person in the group whose behavior they are most puzzled by. Then give each member an opportunity to speak directly to that person and tell what is puzzling about the person's behavior. Require the speaker to *describe* the behavior rather than judge it. The person addressed may either remain silent or respond by explaining the behavior described and the reasons for it. After the two persons interact briefly, proceed to the next member.

Solving the Problem

Once a particular problem within the group has been identified, the following procedures can be used to provide a structured approach to seeking a solution to the problem.

1. Brainstorming.

Write on the board the problem that the class has identified, such as "How can we keep from straying off the topic in our discussions?" Divide the class into small groups of four or five students each. Give the small groups the following instructions:

> (1) During the next 10 minutes you are to come up with as many ideas that might solve this problem as you can. The emphasis is on quantity. Try to generate as many ideas as possible as quickly as you can.

    (2) Don't hold back an idea just because it seems worthless or impractical or kooky.

    (3) If someone else's idea reminds you of a similar idea, say it anyway, even if it isn't completely original.

    (4) Don't discuss or evaluate members' contributions. Evaluation will come later. Just record every idea without comment.

Designate one student in each group to serve as recorder of the ideas generated by all group members. Call time after ten minutes. Ask the groups to review the lists they have made and choose the three solutions that their group feels might be most useful. Give them about five or ten minutes for this step. Then reconvene the total group and have each small group report its three suggestions, writing them on the board as they are given. Finally, have the total class group consider which of the suggestions on the board might be helpful and which they would be willing to adopt.

2. Helping/Hindering.

Working with the total class group in a large circle, write on the board the problem the group has identified and wants to solve. Rephrase the problem in terms of a goal. For example, if the problem is "We stray off the topic in discussions," the goal would be "To stick more closely to the discussion topic." Write the goal on the board and under it draw two columns, one headed "Helping Forces," and the other headed "Hindering Forces." A helping force moves the group toward its goal; a hindering force keeps the group from reaching the goal. Ask the group members to think of all the helping and hindering forces related to this particular goal, and list their ideas in the appropriate columns.

Then go back over the lists and examine each suggestion in detail. Read each helping force and ask students to think of ways it could be strengthened. For example, if they've said that one force that helps keep the group on the topic is for individual members to remind the group when they see the group is straying, ask them how individuals can be encouraged to serve this function—should special "watchdogs" be appointed, perhaps, or should every member just resolve to be more vigilant in this regard?

Then, for each hindering force, ask students to think of how it could be minimized. If, for example, they've said that what keeps them from staying off the topic are the distracting comments of a few students who are not interested in the discussion topic, ask them how this problem could be eliminated—is there some way those persons could be encouraged to be more interested, or is there a way they could be discouraged from making comments that distract the group?

Finally, make a list of the steps the members decide they are willing to take to achieve the goal, steps that will both strengthen helping forces and eliminate hindering forces. At a later classroom meeting, discuss what progress is being made toward the goal.

3. Conflict Reduction.

If the problem identified by the group concerns interpersonal conflict, the suggestions for structured experiences for coping with conflict presented in the next chapter will be useful.

It is not necessary to complete all the activities suggested for all the Stage Two norms. Some of the norms may be more easily achieved than others; some may require less deliberate practice. The teacher will know when a norm has really been adopted by the class when members begin to apply it in all their work, not just during practice activities. The teacher should provide additional structured experiences if this is not happening. But do not wait for complete, consistent mastery; there will be lapses. The important thing is that a solid foundation be laid and that students have a clearer understanding of the behavior and attitudes that are desirable and helpful in working together. When students begin to monitor themselves and each other without waiting for teacher intervention, it is a good sign that the group is ready to move on.

8 STAGE THREE: COPING WITH CONFLICT

"Well, I think it is obvious that you haven't examined the facts! The New Republic says . . ." Susan was beginning her daily harangue at Jay, and Janet started to turn off as usual. But suddenly something strange happened.

"Frankly, I don't care what you think," Lee interrupted. Janet was startled. It was one of the few times Lee had spontaneously spoken in class, and Janet was amazed that he was not only talking, but he was taking on Susan.

"Every day we sit here and you expect us to be interested in what you think," Lee went on. "You obviously don't care what we think. You never listen when anyone else talks. And you never really know what you are talking about!"

"Well, if it weren't for me this whole class would fall apart," Susan replied indignantly. "I'm usually the only one who will say anything. You all just sit here like a bunch of deadheads."

"How can you expect anyone else to talk when every time someone does you go into your old sarcastic routine and cut them down?" Lee continued.

"What's the matter, can't you take it?" Susan asked.

"I could if I wanted to," Lee replied angrily, "but there

are some things I just don't want to bother with—like smallpox and your loud mouth!"

Bruce and Mark cheered. Janet wasn't sure how to react. She felt like cheering too, but she also felt that it wasn't right to be so brutally honest with Susan.

It seemed to Janet that for the last week or so there had been one conflict after another in this class. People like Lee who had not participated actively before were beginning to get involved, but now they were getting into really vicious arguments. For several weeks things had been going beautifully. Discussions had been interesting, and while Susan had still dominated, even Janet had felt freer to take part. But now all of a sudden it was fight, fight, fight. She couldn't figure out what was the matter.

"How are you feeling right now, Susan?" Mr. Stanford asked.

Suddenly Janet knew what the matter was. For the first time in her 10 years as a student she spoke out without raising her hand. "Why are you always asking people how they are feeling?" she said to Mr. Stanford, surprised at the hostility in her voice. "That's what the trouble with this class is. You are always making people say things they don't want to say, making them analyze every little thing. Why don't you just let us work things out ourselves? I'm sure the rest of the class agrees with me that we've been managing nicely for the past few weeks—we've worked together really well. Why don't you just leave us alone?"

The class stared open-mouthed at Janet, aghast at this totally unexpected outburst. But one by one the students started nodding and murmuring—"Yeah, you tell him, Janet"—and as they regained their composure they turned toward Mr. Stanford to see how he'd respond.

Janet's class, which for several weeks had been functioning smoothly and more and more effectively, had entered a new but predictable stage of group development—the

Conflict Stage. What at first appeared to be only minor problems in the students' patterns of interaction reached almost crisis proportions, despite every attempt the teacher made to head them off. The class almost seemed determined to explode—with the previously uninvolved Lee taking on domineering Susan, and reticent and cooperative Janet attacking her teacher. The most complex and bewildering stage of group development was in full swing.

CHARACTERISTICS AND CAUSES OF THE CONFLICT STAGE

That a group whose productivity and cohesiveness have been steadily increasing can suddenly plunge into open expressions of hostility is hard to comprehend at first. We would assume that if we have done all the right things— helping students get acquainted and establishing productive patterns of working together—the group members would become more and more congenial and cooperative. It seems logical that, as members gain skills and experience in working together, they would be less likely to get embroiled in conflict; but in reality the opposite is true.

It is almost inevitable that on the road toward maturity a group will go through a period—sometimes short, sometimes painfully long, depending on how it is handled by the teacher—during which the bickering among members increases and attacks on the teacher become more frequent.

During my early work with group dynamics, I questioned whether a Conflict Stage was virtually inevitable, especially if the teacher had prepared the group properly with getting-acquainted and skill-building activities. My skepticism was dramatically eliminated, however, one evening when I was serving as group dynamics consultant with a group of approximately 20 teachers who had been selected to work together on a long-term curriculum project. The curriculum supervisor had decided that to assure that they would work together most effectively, the group should receive direct help with group development. For the first two or three days everything went superbly. A high degree of cohesiveness was emerging in the group; members got to know one another on a level they had never before achieved with co-workers; and they were thoroughly enjoying working together. I was secretly very pleased with myself for having been instrumental in bringing about this change in the group. The teachers seemed headed toward becoming a very productive working team, and I knew the curriculum project would be far more successful as a result.

Sitting with other leaders of the workshop over dinner on the third day, I was basking in the compliments handed me by my colleagues. The curriculum supervisor was obviously pleased. I remarked casually that many experts in group dynamics would maintain that the group was due for a period of rebellion and conflict. "I guess we've proved them wrong," I said smugly. "If we get through this evening's session without a hitch, we'll have demonstrated that the Conflict Stage is a figment of some expert's imagination."

But we didn't. No sooner had we reconvened than trouble began. Decisions that the group had previously arrived at suddenly were no longer acceptable. Squabbles broke out between people who had, just hours earlier, declared how much they were looking forward to working together. The group began to polarize between the teachers who were more traditional and those who wanted radical changes in the curriculum. Soon, the workshop leaders became the focus of the attacks: "You have been trying to ram ideas down our throats! Why don't you ask us what we want to do rather than telling us? Why must the sessions at this workshop be so highly structured; can't we be more on our own to do what we think needs to be accomplished?" The teachers even complained about the workshop leaders sitting together at meals, away from the participants.

By acknowledging the conflict and dealing with it openly, we were able to resolve many of the problems that came to a head that evening, and the group moved on to become a well developed, highly productive team. Members emerged from their brief Conflict Stage with improved skills and attitudes, and I emerged with a new appreciation for what the experts were saying about the Conflict Stage!

Since then I have noticed that virtually every group I work with enters a period of conflict if they have been successful in going through the previous stages. Some groups, it is true, never get far enough along to enter the Conflict Stage, becoming arrested at some earlier point in their development. If, however, a group remains together and the leader continues to give attention to group dynamics and helps the group move ahead, a period of conflict predictably arises.

Although the reasons for the Conflict Stage are not completely clear, one logical explanation is that if the teacher has been successful in establishing norm #5—confronting problems rather than ignoring them—conflicts that would ordinarily go unexpressed will begin to emerge. Where this norm has not been established, conflicts are suppressed, and the group works at some level of effectiveness without confronting conflicts openly. However, to improve the group's performance, problems must be confronted, which means opening the "can of worms" that will inevitably result in open expression of conflict. The conflict that thus erupts is not "new" conflict, but is merely the open expression of conflicts that were present all the time but were ignored. For example, Lee had been silently fuming about Susan's dominating the group all along, but only after we had worked to establish norm #5 did he confront Susan openly and thus provoke conflict.

Another explanation for the inevitability of the Conflict Stage is that it is the natural result of widespread participation. According to Jay Hall, "One of the most immediately apparent effects of more widespread participation among a group's members is the vast array of divergent ideas and values which surfaces. Disagreements on definitions of goals, differences among strategies for achieving them, interpersonal grievances, and collisions of value all begin to come to the level of group awareness when participation becomes more uniform and freewheeling in groups."[1] Thus, if norms #1 and #2 (responsibility and responsiveness) have been established and more members contribute and encourage others to contribute, conflict may emerge as a result of the diversity of opinions produced. Conflicts are less likely to arise if the only people actively involved are those who agree with one another!

Another reason for the conflict that results after the Norm Establishment Stage is that group members seem to feel the need to challenge and test the teacher's sincerity. For example, the teacher conveys the message, "I want you to share your opinions openly, even if they do not agree with the majority," and so the student sets out to test whether the teacher really means this, sometimes by expressing the most absurd ideas and violent disagreements. Students may even manufacture problems in order to test whether the teacher really welcomes open confrontation of problems.

Sometimes the conflict that erupts following the Norm Establishment Stage is an expression of rebellion against the leadership of the teacher. If group members feel successful at taking responsibility for their own work, they may begin to challenge the teacher's control over classroom activities. When students see that they can do most of the things that teachers did previously, they begin to want to take over. It was the realization that they could work effectively on their own that led the teachers in the in-service workshop on curriculum to ask "Why can't we be more on our own to do what we think

---

[1]Hall, J., and M.S. Williams. "A Comparison of Decision-Making Performances in Established and Ad Hoc Groups." *Journal of Personality and Social Psychology*, 3 (2), page 214.

needs to be accomplished?" and that led Janet to ask her teacher, "Why don't you just let us work things out ourselves?"

If group development is compared with the development of the infant into a mature adult, the Conflict Stage can be seen as comparable to adolescence, in which the young person, having become more competent in coping with the world, struggles to become independent and free of parental control. And like the adolescent, a group in the Conflict Stage usually goes overboard in expressing its rebellion. Instead of quietly accepting more and more responsibility, members often feel a need to assert their independence through rebellion. The term "counter-dependent" is sometimes used to describe members' behavior during this stage. They are not truly independent, but merely wish to counteract the dependency felt in earlier stages.

Finally, the Conflict Stage can be viewed as a natural reaction to increased interpersonal intimacy resulting from group development activities. Getting to know other people well, even though it is a very rewarding experience, can also be unnerving. Students are not used to establishing close relationships with others in their classes; they are not used to becoming a cohesive group. And although they may like the experience in most respects, they may be frightened and bewildered by it also. Thus, they may unconsciously generate conflict within the group to reestablish some distance.

Similarly, successful performance as a classroom group is a new experience for most students. They had probably been used to doing as little as possible, participating as little as necessary, and not enjoying class work too much. But if a group has moved successfully through the Norm Establishment Stage, its members are working together effectively, and are probably enjoying the experience. In order not to appear to have "sold out," students sometimes unconsciously regress to lower levels of productivity and group maturity. Being successful makes them uncomfortable because it is in violation of their previous behavior patterns; so to relieve their anxiety they may unconsciously create conflict within the group to prove that they aren't really all that successful after all.

HELPFUL TEACHER BEHAVIOR
IN THE CONFLICT STAGE

Explain that conflict can be a positive force.

In order to be most useful to a class that is entering the Conflict Stage, you should first examine your own attitudes toward conflict. For many people, conflict is something bad to be avoided at all costs. They see disagreement as evidence that people are not getting along. In a group situation, these persons avoid conflict because they think it gets in the way of efficient work. They worry that the relationships among people in the group may be permanently harmed by conflict. Therefore, they try to create harmony and they avoid, minimize, or gloss over real expressions of hostility or disagreement.

On the other hand, conflict can be seen as a natural result of the interaction of people with divergent values and opinions. From this viewpoint, conflict is an indicator that positive things are happening in the group: people are feeling free to express themselves; more than just a few members are sharing their opinions; and members are committed enough to the goals of the group to become actively involved. When viewed from this perspective, conflict is not something to be avoided or suppressed, but can be a positive force that results from good interpersonal interaction and can lead to high quality group work. Indeed, the research of Hall and Williams[2]

---

[2]*Ibid.*, pages 214-222.

reveals that in high conflict conditions, group members actually tend to generate more creative solutions to problems than in low conflict situations.

In addition, conflict is almost a necessary precondition for change and growth. Kelley and Thibaut[3] have pointed out that only when individuals become aware that their opinions differ from those of other people are they likely to re-examine their ideas and values. This, of course, is one basic justification for group discussion in the classroom. Since education by its very definition requires continual reassessment of one's ideas and values, conflict is an essential ingredient in the process.

Changes in interpersonal relations and personal growth are likewise dependent on conflict. For example, it was only through the conflict that resulted when Lee finally challenged Susan that she was able to examine her impact on other people and alter her behavior. Granted that conflict sometimes leads to cruelty, violence, maliciousness, and other destructive behavior; but these forms of behavior are not synonymous with conflict; they are ways some people respond to a conflict situation. Students can be taught to deal with conflicts constructively, openly confronting their disagreements but not harming other persons in the process.

If the teacher believes that conflict is a positive force, and conveys this attitude to students, the problems of the Conflict Stage are likely to be lessened. It is probably a good idea to discuss in detail with the class your own views about conflict and help students explore theirs. You can help them see that conflict is not inherently bad; it is how people sometimes choose to respond to it that is harmful.

---

[3]Kelley, H.H., and J.W. Thibaut. "Experimental Studies of Group Problem Solving and Process." *Handbook of Social Psychology*. Ed. G. Lindzey. Vol. 2 (1954), pages 735-785.

Provide support and reassurance for students who feel anxious about open expressions of conflict.

Some students are likely to become nervous, even upset, when they see members of the class in conflict with one another. You should indicate to them that you understand their feelings of anxiety, and reassure them that the disagreement will be properly handled and will not result in anyone's being hurt.

A number of students are likely to feel particularly anxious about challenges to the authority of the teacher. A student who has been accustomed to showing "respect" for the teacher and accepting without question control by the teacher is often upset to hear a classmate challenging and rebelling against the teacher. The "respectful" student has depended on the teacher's authority as a source of security, and when that security is threatened the student may become anxious and withdrawn. These students need reassurance that the teacher can cope with criticism from students without going to pieces.

To provide security for these anxious students, you must avoid the impulse to toss aside all control and abolish all limits in response to criticism from some students. A teacher is sometimes tempted to say, "OK, you take over; see if you can do better." Although you must be open to changing classroom procedures in response to students' increased desires for independence, to abdicate all responsibility for the class is likely to throw many students into an emotional tailspin. Extracting and using the positive elements of students' criticism demonstrates that conflict can be constructive.

Don't become more authoritarian.

Although it's important to provide support for students by staying in control of the situation, resist the impulse to panic and tighten up in response to students' criticism. For many teachers, the squabbles and bickering—to say nothing of the challenges to the authority of the teacher—during the Conflict Stage are indications of "misbehavior"; as a result, they impose stricter limits and tighten up classroom management. This will at best temporarily suppress rather than solve the problems students are experiencing; at worst it will heighten the conflict. Try to accept the Conflict Stage philosophically, rather than retaliating against students with harsh discipline. Regard it as an inevitable part of the group's growth toward maturity. Acknowledge and accept the conflict emerging in the group, and help students learn constructive ways of coping with it.

Utilize active listening.

Perhaps the single most important thing teachers can do when students confront them is to *listen*! No solution will ever be satisfactory unless the students feel that they have been heard and understood. Briefly restated, the techniques of active listening as developed in Chapter Four, Establishing Norm 2—Responding to Others, are:

> Look at the speaker.
>
> Give nonverbal signals that show you are listening (e.g., nodding your head).
>
> Show you have understood.
>
> Don't be afraid of silences.
>
> Do not shift the focus from the speaker to yourself.
>
> Encourage the speaker to continue talking.
>
> Show you have understood by summarizing or restating the speaker's remarks from time to time.

During the Conflict Stage you will need to utilize active listening continuously. In addition, you will want to be sure that students have also mastered this skill. It might be helpful at this point in your group's development to repeat some of the listening activities with your students.

Respond to the feelings underlying the students' words.

In conjunction with active listening, you need to let students who confront you know that you understand and accept the feelings that lie behind their actual words. Imagine that Sarah yells at you "Why do you pick on me all the time?" To paraphrase the actual words she used is of little help in dealing with the conflict. You must try to determine what feelings probably underlie the words and show you have understood and accepted these feelings. A useful response to this outburst would probably be "You seem angry with me, Sarah. Can you tell me more about what's bugging you?"

Often students camouflage their hostility by voicing it as a question, as Sarah did above. It's a real temptation to answer the question rather than reflecting the feelings that the question expresses. But answering the literal meaning of the question does little to resolve the conflict and may actually increase it. If you replied to Sarah by answering her question— "I wouldn't have to speak to you so often, Sarah, if you weren't always distracting us"—she would be likely to feel even more annoyed and might look for other ways to get back at you. On the other hand, if you showed understanding of Sarah's feelings—"You seem pretty annoyed with me, Sarah. What is making you so angry?"—you would stay in communication and might work out a solution to the conflict.

Responding to feelings is also a useful approach for students to utilize in their conflicts with one another. Demonstrate this technique to them, let them practice it in role-playing situations, and then encourage them to utilize it whenever conflicts arise in the classroom.

STRUCTURED APPROACHES FOR COPING WITH CONFLICT

1. Sending "I" Messages.

An "I" message is a statement of how something someone is doing makes you feel: "I feel annoyed when I see you throw paper on the floor." A "You" message—the way most of us habitually communicate with people (especially with those we have authority over)—tells what's wrong with the person: "You are messy"; "You are inconsiderate of other people"; "You shouldn't be so thoughtless"; "Why can't you be more careful?" An "I" message gives accurate information about the impact a person is having on you, whereas a "You" message is an attempt to label or blame the person.

Psychologist Thomas Gordon, whose Effectiveness Training Associates have helped countless parents and teachers improve their communication with young people, points out that:

> A teacher who sends an I-message is taking responsibility for his own inner condition (listening to *himself*) and assuming responsibility for being open enough to share this assessment of himself with a student; secondly, I-messages leave the responsibility for the student's behavior with the student. At the same time, I-messages avoid the negative impact that accompanies you-messages, freeing the student to be considerate and helpful, not resentful, angry, and devious.
>
> Students will look at this teacher (who sends I-messages) as a real person, because he is developing the inner security to expose his feelings, first to himself and then to others—to show himself as a person *capable* of feeling disappointment, hurt,

anger, fear. He will be seen by students as genuine, someone with weaknesses, a vulnerable person, even at times a person who feels inadequate and frightened—someone very like the students.[4]

During conflict, to a certain extent it is helpful to simply avoid statements that begin with "You" ("You're never willing to settle down to work on time") and attempt to begin statements with "I feel . . . " ("I feel discouraged when I realize how little work we've gotten done this week").

Students will find the "I-message" approach valuable in dealing with conflicts, and should be taught to utilize it. Explain the difference between describing the other person ("You" message) and reporting one's own feelings ("I" message), and encourage them to practice replacing "You" messages with "I" messages when conflicts erupt in the classroom.

2. Negotiating No-Lose Solutions.

Conflict is usually the result of two or more parties wanting different things. Most people assume that when conflicts are solved one person "wins" and the other "loses." They would say, for example, that teachers have two choices in a conflict—to "win" over the students by invoking their authority, or to "lose" by giving in and letting the students do what they want. You may remember from your days as a beginning teacher that many colleagues warned you that if you didn't keep the upper hand ("win" in conflicts with students) you would find yourself with the kids running all over you ("losing"). This either-or thinking is not helpful in the process

---

[4]Copyright © 1974 by Thomas Gordon. From the book *Teacher Effectiveness Training*, published by Peter H. Wyden, a division of David McKay Company, Inc. Reprinted by permission of the publisher.

of conflict reduction. There is a third alternative—to seek a solution that both the teacher and the students will be comfortable with. This might be called a "no-lose" approach, or a consensual model for conflict resolution. It assumes that a solution can be found which will meet the needs of both parties, so that neither party will have to "give in."

The first step is, of course, to identify the conflict. For example, the teacher might start by stating simply, "We seem to be experiencing a conflict here. I'm eager to have you do some work on grammar in these programmed texts, but you wish to continue the discussion on slang. Is that right?"

The next step is to ask for possible solutions. It is helpful to encourage students to contribute solutions first, to show them that you are genuinely interested in their ideas and are not going to ramrod through your own solution. They might suggest, "Maybe we can just forget the grammar work; it's boring anyhow" or "Why don't we leave the grammar exercises until tomorrow?" or "Why don't we do the grammar exercises as homework?" After you have drawn out of the group all their solutions, you may add your own suggestions, such as "I think you've spent enough time on the discussion on slang; why don't you stop for now and continue again tomorrow if you still want to talk about it then?"

Then, examine the alternatives to see whether any of them are acceptable to both parties. If you can't live with some of their suggestions, explain why. "Your idea about doing the exercises as homework is a good one, but I can't let you take the books home because I use them with the sixth-hour class also." As each alternative is analyzed, it is likely that other alternatives may emerge or that modifications can be made so that one suggestion becomes a satisfactory solution to both parties.

When a solution has been discovered, check carefully to make sure that both parties in the conflict are willing to commit themselves to it. The process will break down unless both sides honestly report whether they can live with the proposed solution.

Negotiation of this type is not unusual between parties of equal power. Husbands and wives, for example, continually explore alternatives that both can accept. But in the classroom, where teachers have more power than the students, it is theoretically possible for teachers to "win" every conflict and impose their solution on the students simply because the teacher is "the boss." We all know, however, that imposed solutions rarely bring satisfactory results because resentment is stirred up. If, when conflict erupts between students and teacher, the teacher deliberately refrains from imposing a solution and instead invites students to find a mutually acceptable solution, students may follow this pattern when conflicts erupt among themselves. This is the kind of solution to a conflict that Shakespeare had in mind when he wrote, "A peace is of the nature of a conquest; for then both parties nobly are subdued, and neither party loser."

3. The Four-Step Strategy.

Students should be given practice in combining the techniques suggested above into a systematic, four-step approach to dealing with a conflict. The first step is to use active listening to determine what the other person is thinking and feeling. The second step is to convey to the other person that you understand and accept the feelings that are reflected in the person's statement. The third step is to describe to the other person your own feelings, using an "I" instead of a "You" message ("I'm annoyed that you don't seem interested in doing the work necessary for us to complete our work.") Finally, you enter into negotiation of a no-lose solution to the conflict.

4. Role Reversal.

When a conflict arises between two people, suggest that they exchange roles temporarily. That is, for a few minutes they each try to act the way they think the other person would.

This change in roles gives both parties a change in perspective and a deeper understanding of the point of view of the other.

Here's an example of how an eighth-grade teacher I know used this technique:

"Miss Johnson, do you *have* to be gone again? It's always so boring when you're gone because the subs don't ever do anything interesting," complained Dora.

"From the reports I've had, you don't cooperate very well with the substitutes," Miss Johnson replied.

"Hey, this is a conflict!" Denise suddenly piped up from the back of the room.

"You're right, Denise," Miss Johnson admitted. "And what can we do to solve it?"

"Let's try role reversal," suggested Mark enthusiastically.

Hands popped up. "I want to be Miss Johnson!" "No, let me!" "Let me!"

"All right, Elaine, why don't you play me and I'll be. you," said Miss Johnson, moving to Elaine's seat.

Elaine giggled a minute, then sat on the teacher's desk and crossed her legs in a remarkable imitation of Miss Johnson. "Class," she began, in only a slightly exaggerated tone of voice, "I am going to be gone again Friday for another day of work with the curriculum development team."

The class, including Miss Johnson playing Elaine, groaned loudly. "Why do you have to be gone so much?" asked Dora again.

"You all know," said Elaine, "that I am helping to write the new social studies curriculum. And you've all said that you're enjoying the new activities that I've been trying out in class."

"Yes," said Tod, "the new lessons are great, but you leave us such awful boring stuff to do when you're gone. Why can't we do the simulation game you were telling us about while you're gone?"

"But I've worked hard writing that simulation game and

I want to be here to see how it works out," replied Elaine, playing the role of teacher.

Miss Johnson was startled. She had taught these kids to use role reversal, but she had never believed the strategy would work so well that Elaine could voice her very thoughts.

"But surely we don't have to do anything as boring as those study sheets you left last time," Rex begged.

"What would you rather do while I'm gone?" asked Elaine, now so involved in the part that the exaggerated mannerisms had disappeared.

Suggestions poured out of the students, ranging from free study days to writing their own simulation game. Within 10 minutes a compromise had been reached and the problem, while not completely resolved, was considerably alleviated.

Role reversal is useful for conflicts between students as well as between teacher and students. It can serve as a quick intervention method in heated arguments and other conflicts. Instruct the two students to exchange places and continue the argument, each taking the role of the other person. After a few minutes, have them return to their original roles and talk about what they learned from the role reversal.

5. You Say/I Say.

This conflict reduction mechanism is useful because it assures that the parties involved are communicating clearly and listening closely to one another. The rules are simple: each speaker must first summarize, to the satisfaction of the other person, the point that the other person was making. The speaker may then—and only then—go on to make his or her own statement. If the other person was not satisfied with the summary, before going on the speaker must ask questions of the other person until an accurate summary results.

When locked in conflict with a student, the teacher can apply this approach either unilaterally or bilaterally. That is, the teacher can attempt to summarize what the student is saying before replying, in hopes that this will lead to resolution; or the teacher can request that the student also summarize before responding. It is usually more effective to implement bilateral summarizing.

When a conflict arises, the teacher can say something like this: "Randy, we seem to be in pretty serious disagreement over this thing. I wonder if you would be willing to summarize what I'm saying before you respond to me, and I'll agree to do the same for you. That way we'll be able to understand one another more accurately. Okay? Then, I'll begin: You say that I ought to postpone the test until next Thursday because most people haven't finished the reading assignment. Is that right? Okay, then I say that I feel you've had plenty of time to complete the assignment before now. Now it's your turn. Summarize what I said before you reply to it."

"You Say/I Say" sentences can begin with phrases like, "I'm not sure I understand. Do you mean. . . ?"; "Are you saying that. . . ?"; "Do I understand you to say. . . ?"; or "Can I assume that you mean. . . ?" Initially the method may seem awkward and stilted, but as you put it into practice you will find that it has an almost miraculous effect on arguments, and ultimately you can fall into a more natural question and answer pattern.

For further practice in the "You Say/I Say" approach, activities #6 (*Responding to the Previous Speaker*, page 135) and #7 (*Practice in Restating*, page 136) from the Norm Establishment Stage may be used again. Then when conflicts arise between students in the classroom, you can remind them to utilize these techniques in responding to one another. You can also point out to students that this approach can be valuable for solving conflicts outside of school: "If there is someone you like, but argue with frequently, explain the rules of 'You Say/I Say' to that person, and the next time the two of you get into a fight, ask the person to follow the rules. If you don't know the person well enough or if you think it would be embarrassing to set up rules for an argument, you can usually influence the conflict simply by using the 'You Say/I Say' method yourself. Most of us imitate the person we are talking to. If that person shouts, we shout; if the other person calls us names, we respond in kind. And if the person tries to understand what we're saying, we usually do the same, too. So if you put the method to work unilaterally by summarizing what the other person has said before you respond, that person will probably start doing the same."

6.   The 3R Strategy.

Often, people in a conflict are not really certain what they are arguing over, or they are arguing over something which neither party has the power to change. Using the 3R Strategy—Resentment, Request, Recognition—reveals that a conflict is far easier to resolve than was originally assumed. It was this strategy that I adapted for use in the conflict between Linda and Bob (see page 202).

To apply this strategy, one person in the conflict begins by stating what the other person has done to make the speaker feel *resentful*. The other person must listen without interrupting. Then this person in turn states what he or she resents about the first person, while the first person listens without interrupting.

Then each of the parties to the conflict states a *request*. They tell in turn what the other person could do in order to make them feel better and to solve the problem.

The *recognition* step has two parts. First, the people involved indicate which of the other person's requests they would be willing to meet; this must be done in a spirit of compromise (similar to the *No-Lose Negotiation* suggested previously, page 238). They may need to continue negotiating for a few minutes until a satisfactory plan of action is decided on.

Then the people in turn make statements about the things they recognize as likeable or admirable in the other person. This final step helps assure that the two parties acknowledge that each of them sees positive as well as annoying qualities in the other.

7. Third-Party Mediation.

The role of the mediator in a conflict is not to identify who is "right" and who is "wrong" (as many teachers tend to do), but to help the two parties arrive at a mutually satisfactory solution. Allen P. Main and Albert E. Roark[5] have developed the mediation procedure that follows.

The first step in this method of resolving conflicts is to explain to the persons involved that it is likely that a mutually agreeable solution can be worked out, and that you're willing to help them work toward it. Make clear that you are *not* willing to take sides in the conflict or set yourself up as a judge, but will help them work toward a solution that both of them can live with. Also make clear that to arrive at a mutually satisfactory solution, both of them will have to be flexible and willing to compromise.

The second step is to have the parties, one at a time, describe the conflict. Encourage them to focus on what the situation looks like at present, rather than reciting a long list of past grievances. Have them stick to the content of the conflict; a description of feelings will come in a later step. If they tend to interrupt one another or are not listening carefully, ask each to summarize the other's position before responding.

The third step is to have the parties explain how the conflict makes them feel. Since most people aren't in the habit of discussing their feelings openly, you may need to ask questions to encourage the two persons to describe in detail how they feel about the situation.

---

[5]Main, Allen P. and Albert E. Roark. "A Consensus Method to Reduce Conflict." *The Personnel and Guidance Journal*, Vol. 53, June 1975, pp. 754-759.

The fourth step is to have both persons tell in turn what they would like as an outcome to the conflict—that is, what would be the "ideal state" from their point of view. As mediator, you should encourage them to arrive at a description of the ideal state that both agree on and would be willing to work toward.

The fifth step is to have the two parties acknowledge changes that each is willing to make in order to bring about the desired situation. As mediator you may have to remind both sides that they may have to give in a bit in order to assure that the solution is mutually acceptable. Sometimes the persons involved in the conflict overlook possible alternatives, and you should feel free to suggest them. But it is essential that both parties genuinely agree to whatever solution is suggested.

The sixth and final step is to draw up a list of the measures both parties agree to take in order to implement the decisions reached in step five. This plan of action should include provision for checking back with the mediator to evaluate how well the solution is being carried out.

The two parties experiencing conflict do not have to be individuals, of course. It is possible to apply the procedure when two groups are in conflict. For example, in one of my college classes several people became upset because others were using obscene language in the class. The people accused of using "bad" language were incensed, maintaining that the complainers were attempting to curtail their freedom of speech.

To help these two groups resolve their conflict, I utilized the *Third-Party Mediation* procedure. Since it was not initially clear which side all the people in the class were on, I had members form a continuum indicating what position they took on the issue of "bad" language in the classroom, ranging from total freedom of expression on the one extreme to total elimination of profanity on the other. Most of the class, as you might expect, fell very much in the middle. But at both extremes there was a small group of adherents of those positions. I asked these persons to form two clusters at the front of the room and I worked with the two groups using the six steps that Roark and Main suggest for working with individuals. The rest of the class observed the process, sharing insights that could be helpful in resolving the conflict and offering possible alternative solutions during the appropriate phase. The issue was complex and laden with emotion and no simple solution was possible. Ultimately one group agreed to be somewhat more prudent in their use of four-letter words if the other group would try to be less critical.

8.   Intergroup Meeting.

This is a structured procedure for helping two conflicting groups examine their perceptions of each other and their assumptions about how the other group perceives them. This strategy is especially useful when a class becomes polarized between "liberals" and "conservatives," "hippies" and "greasers," blacks and whites, highly motivated students and "goof-offs," etc.

Ask all the class members to join either of the two conflicting groups. If some students insist that they do not belong with either group, suggest that they serve as neutral observers. Seat the two conflicting groups in circles as far away from each other as possible. It is best if they can be separated enough that the groups cannot overhear one another—in different rooms if possible.

Give each group three long sheets of newsprint or butcher paper and a felt-tip marker. Have each group draw up the following lists:

List #1   Characteristics the members think describe their group; that is, their own perception of themselves, not how they think others would describe them.

List #2   Characteristics the members think the other group would say they have; for example, the "hippie" group would list

what they think the "greaser" group would
say about the "hippie" group.

List #3   Characteristics the members think describe the other group; for example, the
"hippies" would list the characteristics
they think the "greasers" have.

The three lists should be made independently by each group,
with no communication between groups.

Then bring the groups together. Ask a member of one
group to read off its first list (members' perception of selves).
Do not let members of the other group argue or respond; any
comments should be limited to questions necessary for clarification. Then have a member of the second group read its
first list. Proceed in this manner, alternating groups, until all
the lists have been read. Then ask each group to meet again in
private to discuss questions such as:

How is your group's image of itself different from the
other group's image of you (your list one versus their
list three)?

What behavior on the part of members of your group
may have led to the discrepancy between the lists?
That is, what have you done to cause the other group
to think you are different from what you are?

What have members of the other group done to
contribute to your misperception of them?

After the two groups have discussed these questions
separately, seat all students in one large circle, including the
neutral members who have been acting as observers. Make
sure that students sit randomly, not with one group facing the
other across the circle. Ask students to talk over ways members
of each group could behave differently in the future to reduce
misconceptions.

Whatever the causes of the Conflict Stage, it is a very real phenomenon in groups that have successfully completed the Norm Establishment Stage. It is certainly the most trying period in the group's life for teacher and students alike. But properly handled, this period can lead to increased interpersonal skills on the part of students as they learn constructive ways of grappling with conflicts, and it can result in a still higher level of group productivity and maturity.

9 STAGE FOUR: PRODUCTIVITY

"Susan," asked Janet, "do you really think our letter will change the mayor's mind?"

"Well, I can't be certain, but from all I could find out about him, he gets a big charge out of what he calls 'school children becoming involved in civic affairs.' And if Lee's detailed research on the dangers to bicycle riders doesn't get to him, I don't know what will. As they always tell us in debating—nothing argues louder than the facts."

"Good," Janet replied. "Lee, have you checked over our letter to be sure we summarized all of your research accurately?"

"Yeah," Lee said. "It's all fine, except that this sentence we changed from compound to complex makes it sound as if the bike rider is endangered because of the stop light, and it really should be in spite of the light."

"Okay, I'll change that," Janet said.

"Are you sure Mo. is the correct way to abbreviate Missouri?" Bruce asked. "I keep getting mixed up since the post office changed it."

"I'm pretty sure it is," Janet replied, "but maybe we'd better ask Mr. Stanford to be sure. Call him over here, somebody. While we're waiting for him, does anybody else see *anything about the letter that needs improving? This letter has got to be absolutely perfect so that the mayor can't ignore what we're trying to say about the bikeway proposal. Shari, how about you?"*

"No, you've already put in the changes I wanted," Shari replied. *"The part about the financial benefits that will result— remember?"*

"Then after we get this thing about Missouri figured out, I guess we're ready for Bruce to type it," Janet said. *"Are you going to have time to do it tonight, Bruce?"*

It was hard to believe that this was the same class that Janet had thought just a few months earlier was "pretty bad," filled with the school troublemakers and dumb kids. They've learned to work together cooperatively, and their squabbles with one another and with the teacher have diminished. Mutual respect abounds; members participate actively in ways that are most appropriate for them; and the unique contributions of each person are valued. The group can work effectively on its own, but members feel free to consult the teacher when they need an outside resource. They have arrived at the Productivity Stage.

CHARACTERISTICS OF THE PRODUCTIVITY STAGE

This is what all the struggle has been toward. The class has become a mature working unit, possessing the skills and attitudes necessary for effective interaction in learning activities. Students can work together to accomplish a variety of learning tasks and can deal with disagreement and interpersonal conflict in constructive ways.

However, an especially important characteristic of the

Productivity Stage is that the group's attention seems to alternate between the task at hand and the interpersonal needs of members. At times students may be enthusiastically committed to achieving their goals (in the classroom this usually involves a subject-matter task) and they work together as smoothly as a well oiled machine. At other times, they may be more concerned about their interpersonal relationships and may have trouble mustering much interest in the task the group is supposed to be working on.

Some of Janet's journal entries give a clear picture of what a group is like when it is giving more attention to interpersonal needs than task needs:

> *The past few days I have been happy with our class pleasure-wise, but not learning-wise. I really started thinking about it when Shari told me how much she hates our class sometimes. She says she likes the kids, but as I agree, we often don't get anything done. I enjoy coming to class, because we do different things and the kids are great, but we don't ever accomplish a task that Mr. Stanford gives us. It bothers me and others, I know, so it's really no use bringing it up because we all know what's wrong. No one has much of an urge to correct it. . . . Mr. Stanford seems very displeased with our class, and I don't blame him! We have accomplished absolutely nothing in about the last five days. . . . I look forward to this class just because I have a good time here, but we're not accomplishing anything Mr. Stanford wants us to. I am enjoying Science Fiction a lot as a whole. In fact, I like it the best of all the English courses I've taken. There's pretty much work but the assignments are kind of fun and interesting, too.*

Janet acknowledges that class is pleasant, but it is also frustrating to her, since she is a highly motivated student who is accustomed to working hard on subject-matter tasks and doing a minimum of interacting with other students. It is interesting to note that Janet acknowledges that the group members "all know what's wrong," but that "no one has much of an urge to correct it." That is, they have the skills necessary for productive work on a task, but during this brief period they would rather put their energy into improving their relationships with each other. It is also significant that even though Janet is frustrated and perhaps guilty about the group's lack of task-related activity, she nevertheless is enjoying the class and assignments. This may be reassuring if a teacher is concerned that a class may be wasting time during the periods of emphasis on relationships rather than on content goals.

Both are, of course, essential to the group's success: if members are unwilling or unable to undertake subject-matter tasks, their reason for being together is unfulfilled; but if they do not give attention to their interpersonal relationships, their effectiveness on subject-matter tasks will be reduced by conflicts and unmet emotional needs. A balance between the two emphases needs to be struck. The periods of attention to relationships rather than content are very valuable to the students' personal growth. Growth in social skills and individual emotional development are an important part of what education is all about, and thus these periods should be seen as valuable in their own right, not regarded just as a hiatus in subject-matter learning to be tolerated by a nervous or impatient teacher.

The Productivity Stage often brings with it increased intimacy between students and between students and the teacher. The teacher has been disclosing personal information and feelings during the Conflict Stage, and has been showing interest in and acceptance of the students. This sometimes leads students to reevaluate their image of the teacher and their relationship to the teacher. For perhaps the first time, they start to become emotionally close to a teacher, and frequently they aren't sure how to handle these feelings.

Mark H., in Janet's class, experimented with calling me by my first name—partly to test me to see if I'd get mad, and partly as a way of signaling that he was moving emotionally closer to me. Here's how Janet saw it:

> Friday, before class, I was really shocked. Mr. Stanford walked in and someone said, "Hi, Gene!" and he said "Hi!" Most teachers get very offended when a student calls them by their first name. I think it's really cool this way. I feel much closer to a person whom I call by first name. I don't really think I'll ever say, "Hi, Gene," because I have a lot of respect for Mr. Stanford as a person and as a teacher. I feel that a teacher should be called "Mr." unless one has had a further acquaintance with him other than a teacher-student relationship.

Students also develop increased intimacy among themselves during those periods when they concentrate on interpersonal relations.

> Mr. Stanford wasn't here today, so we had Mrs. W. as a substitute. Our discussion today consisted mostly of dirty jokes. I didn't get half of them. At one time, the whole class had to explain it. It was a lot of fun today. Shari, Bruce, and I had an unusual conversation on sex. Bruce isn't as innocent as I thought he was. Shari and I were hysterical, because of the way Bruce described everything. He is really funny!!!

> I was talking to Jay in class and he shocked me. He said that he used to be so quiet in classes last year. Now he's our leader. I can't believe that he could let someone else take the lead (last year) when he's so smart.

> Mr. Stanford is splitting us up now. He says we're spending too much time socializing and not enough on classwork. He says I can't sit near Shari anymore. I'm so mad. I love her and now I won't get to talk to her much any more except in the halls. That was how Shari and I got so close—being in this class together— I wish that we didn't have to be moved.

Those of us who decry the sense of alienation and separation that schools generally produce in students (as described in Marc Robert's *Loneliness in the Schools*, for example) are pleased to see students deepening their relationships during the Productivity Stage. However, if the increased intimacy is developing at the expense of work on subject-matter tasks, the teacher may have to take some steps to right the balance (as I did) so that neither aspect is sacrificed.

HELPFUL TEACHER BEHAVIOR IN THE PRODUCTIVITY STAGE

Help the group maintain its skills.

.To maintain the group's skills at the high level members have achieved usually requires using some of the approaches suggested previously in relation to seeing and solving problems. In general, training exercises are no longer necessary, unless specific weaknesses are detected for which exercises might be appropriate. Normally, merely identifying and talking over the problems students are having is adequate to get a group in the Productivity Stage back to their optimal level of effectiveness.

Be prepared for temporary regression.

Occasionally, a group in this stage of development will temporarily regress, manifesting symptoms such as withdrawal, lack of participation, chaos, lack of organization, hostility, and conflict that are reminiscent of earlier stages. Periods of regression are most likely to occur when some special event interrupts the normal classroom routine. Frequently, for example, a group will lose ground in its developmental process when a vacation period occurs. An interruption of even three or four days during the Thanksgiving holidays, for instance, can cause the class to slip back into earlier patterns of interaction. Similarly, if one or more new members are added to the class, the students may need a little while to get readjusted to the new composition of the group.

Regression also occurs when students who have been working in small groups that have stayed intact for several weeks—working on a special project, perhaps—are brought back together into the total group or are reassigned to new small groups. Following any unusual occurrence of this nature, the teacher will want to take special care to help students become reacquainted and adjusted to the new situation.

Expect alternation between working on tasks and working on relationships.

Handling the swings from task-orientation to relationship-orientation that generally take place during this stage takes patience and skill. On the one hand, the teacher doesn't want to discourage students from enjoying and deepening their relationships with one another. As educators we have a serious obligation to help students master social skills and grow in social and emotional dimensions as well as academic ones. On the other hand, this is a period when the class is best prepared to do effective work on subject-matter tasks, and it is a pity not to take advantage of the opportunity. Many students get uncomfortable when the class spends too much time on things other than work on subject-matter goals.

A way to meet both tasks and social-emotional goals is to devise learning activities for the group that link their personal concerns with the content skills. In the episode which opened this chapter, for example, Janet's class was writing business letters about issues the students were personally involved in. Janet and some of her classmates had been discussing spontaneously their annoyance with the mayor for opposing a proposal to spend public funds on a system of bike paths through the city. I allowed the students to continue their interaction on this issue but, at the same time, encouraged them to gain practice in rhetoric and composition by having them write a letter of protest to the mayor. It was a logical outgrowth of their talk about the problem, and it was excellent training in the skills I wanted them to learn in my English class. Thus, I was able to satisfy the need for work on course content without suppressing the students' need to interact closely with one another. (An excellent source of help in planning activities that combine personal concerns with subject matter is *Clarifying Values through Subject Matter*, by Merrill Harmin, Howard Kirschenbaum, and Sidney B. Simon.)

LEARNING ACTIVITIES FOR THE PRODUCTIVE GROUP

Once a class has successfully developed into a productive group, the range of learning activities that can be satisfactorily undertaken widens considerably. Whereas many teaching methods are almost bound to fail with an undeveloped group—role-playing, for example—these activities will usually be undertaken enthusiastically by a group that has reached the Productivity Stage. The activities that follow utilize the students' newly developed skills of working together effectively.

1. Small Group Projects.

If ever there were a traditional use for dividing a class into groups, this—independent work on projects—is it. In fact, many educators imply that this is the *only* legitimate use for groups within the classroom. Although I see other uses for small groupings, organizing group projects is an excellent activity for a class in the Productivity Stage. In this approach, groups of from four to eight students undertake projects on topics of their choice—often sub-topics of a larger issue that the whole class is studying. Each group conducts independent investigations without the direct supervision of the teacher. After several days (or several weeks) of library research, discussion, and passing of materials back and forth, each group reports its findings to the total class.

This method has a number of advantages. It allows students to choose topics they are interested in and, hence, their involvement is likely to be fairly high. It also provides for a form of division of labor within the total class which gives students the opportunity to utilize their individual skills and talents. It also promotes independence and encourages students to take responsibility for their own learning.

However, the reporting back to the total group can be very tiresome if it is nothing more than having a representative of a small group stand before the class and drone through a report, while the rest of the class squirms or snores. Unless the small groups have uncovered information that the rest of the class perceives as vital to the achievement of its goals, I suggest dispensing with the reporting procedure altogether. Plan the small group work as an end in itself and provide, as follow-up, opportunities for students to sit in a circle and ask one another questions about their projects if they wish.

2. Short-Term Small Group Discussions.

My favorite way to use small groups in the classroom is to have them discuss a question or work on a task during part of a class period. For me, a very comfortable format for the class period is to open with a teacher-centered introduction (which I like to call a "warm up"), identifying the topic and giving the class instructions. I then divide the class at random into groups consisting of four or five students and put them to work on a clearly defined task (it may be one of the group development activities, or it may be a subject-matter task). After 20 minutes or so, I reconvene the class into one large circle and, through a teacher-led discussion, we pool the conclusions that the various groups reached and come to further conclusions together. This three-part division is a convenient way to organize any class period: a warm-up phase in which students are introduced to the day's work, an activity period in which they perform the task, and an integration period for drawing conclusions and examining implications.

3. Simulations.

Often, simply discussing an issue doesn't give students sufficient insight into the way the people involved actually think and feel, especially if the students have not had much personal experience related to the topic. Simulation can give students a second-hand experience (the next best thing to direct experience) which will make their discussion of the topic more meaningful.

For example, Janet's class was slated to read a short story entitled "The Shelter," in which the chief character, having been the only person in his community with the foresight to build a fallout shelter, has to choose which of his friends—if any—to admit to the shelter when the air-raid sirens start wailing, knowing that for every person he admits he reduces his own chance of survival because of the limited supplies of food and water. Before I assigned the story to the class, I gave the following assignment: "Imagine that you had built an air-raid shelter and you had to decide which members of this class you would admit, if any, considering that for every person you admit you reduce your own chances for survival by x number of days." Since the class was a well-developed group, I was able to allow an open discussion of the question. With a less mature group I would probably require the students to write down their decisions but we might not discuss them.

After the group had grappled with this painful decision, I assigned "The Shelter." Here's how Janet described her reaction:

> *We were supposed to have read "The Shelter" for today. It was the best thing I ever read!! I could "feel" the whole story. I could hear what was running through the people's minds. It was just super!! As our class discovered, it's easier to understand and have feelings for certain things when you have first-hand evidence and experience.*

Elaborate simulations and simulation games have been devised for teaching a wide range of concepts, such as "Ghetto," which depicts the forces affecting a disadvantaged minority-group member, "Dangerous Parallel," which explores alternatives for handling an international crisis similar to Korea, and "Napoli," which simulates certain political processes. Simulations require a high degree of interaction among students, and are best undertaken by a well developed group. Good sources of information about simulations are *Simulation Games for the Social Studies Classroom*, by William Nesbitt, Thomas Crowell; *Simulation Games in Learning*, by S. Boocock and E.O. Schild, Sage; and *The Guide to Simulation Games for Education and Training*, by D. Zuckerman and R. Horn.

4. Role-Playing.

A well developed classroom group is essential for role-playing and, when it is used with a well developed group, role-playing is one of the most effective methods of learning. Instead of just talking about issues, students act them out, gaining insight through trying to actually "be" the people involved. In this regard, role-playing is closely related to simulations; in general, however, simulations set up carefully structured situations, whereas role-playing gives students freedom and flexibility to develop the situations the way they want.

Role-playing is also a useful way to rehearse social skills and communication skills learned in the classroom. For example, students in a class that has been learning how to draw out a speaker rather than arguing could practice this technique by role-playing arguments with their parents. Excellent resources for the teacher who wishes to undertake role-playing with a class are: *Value Exploration Through Role-Playing*, by Robert C. Hawley; *Role-Playing Methods in the Classroom*, by M. Chesler and R. Fox; *Role Playing for Social Values*, by F. Shaftel and G. Shaftel; and *Human Interaction in Education*, by G. Stanford and A. Roark.

5.   Adaptations of Group Development Activities.

Many of the activities described earlier in this book as useful for developing the classroom group, particularly during the Orientation and Norm Establishment Stages, can be successfully adapted to subject-matter topics. For example, the format of the following activities can be used for discussions during the Productivity Stage: *Double Circles* (page 61), *Voting Questions* (page 63), *Forced Choice* (page 65), *Continuum* (page 66), *Round Robin* (page 68), *Forced Contribution* (page 88), and *Mystery Games* (page 89). For discussion of controversial issues, students can be grouped in pairs or triads and instructed to follow the active listening guidelines presented earlier (page 132).

6.   Outside-the-Classroom Projects.

Students can be encouraged to undertake projects that get them involved in the world beyond the walls of the classroom. These projects might involve research into social problems through interviews, surveys, and observation, or they could focus on social action, through publicizing problems, influencing public opinion, writing letters, speaking to civic groups, etc. The important ingredient in this kind of project is that a group of students who share a common concern work together to accomplish their purpose.

A wealth of suggestions for projects (such as "Students set up and publicize a service whereby older women help new mothers in the community"), complete with full details and suggestions for implementing them, can be found in *Laboratory Practices in Citizenship: Learning Experiences in the Community*, an obscure publication of the Citizenship Education Project at Teachers College, Columbia University. Don't let the stuffy title and 1958 publication date put you off; this is an excellent resource for teachers of all subjects.

Another good resource is *The Leader's Guide for Social Action*, by D.M. Paine and D. Martinez. This small book will help students act on their concerns about pollution, economic problems, political issues, and many of the other areas that Ralph Nader-backed groups have investigated.

7.   Commercial Materials with Appropriate Activities.

An excellent set of group activities on topics such as loneliness, values, futures, woman and man, and evil—suitable for both English and Social Studies classes—can be found in *Possibilities for Reading and Relating* by M. Sweet, C. Blankenship, and B. Stanford.

Another set of materials that tells the teacher how to structure group activities to help students learn about topics they are concerned about is *Becoming: A Course in Human Relations*, by C.R. Cromwell, W. Ohs, A. Roark, and G. Stanford.

Rarely does a teacher work with a class so pleasant, so cooperative, or so enthusiastic as a class in the Productivity Stage of group development. But nirvana hasn't been reached and, of course, won't be. In order to maintain this level of effectiveness, the teacher cannot abandon group development activities. Attention must continually be given to assessing the process of the group and analyzing interaction, although it will take far less time and effort now than in the previous stages.

10 STAGE FIVE: TERMINATION

"Mr. Stanford, this is a waste of time," Shari announced. "In fact, this whole course has been a waste of time. We haven't learned a thing about English, and next fall when we have Mrs. Kaplan we're all going to be behind."

"Yeah, it's been the biggest waste of a whole wasteful year," Lee chimed in.

"How do you feel knowing that this is the last week of class?" asked Mr. Stanford.

"Great! Free at last!" Lee cheered.

"Really?" Mr. Stanford probed.

Lee squirmed a little. "Well, I am going to miss the kids," he said slowly, looking around the class. "I mean, this is about the nicest class I've ever been in. Like, kids in my other classes are all stuck up. We had some fun in here—like sending that letter to the mayor and getting invited to meet with him at City Hall."

"Yeah, and remember the time we did that shelter thing—about who you'd leave out? That was something!" Bruce added.

"I think that this has been the most valuable class I've ever been in," Janet said. "In all our other English classes we read books about communication, but here we really learned to communicate."

"I'll agree that it has been good getting to know everybody and learning to work together like we did," Shari replied. "But I don't think I've learned anything I can use anywhere else. For example, when you learn to write compositions, you know you'll be able to write better for other classes. But learning to work with this one group of people—where has it gotten us? We'll all separate after this week, so why did we bother to do it? It's like what happened in this class was a freaky, you know, unique thing that's soon going to be over and won't happen again . . . at least I can't make it happen again. We're going to go into Mrs. Kaplan's class next year and we aren't going to know how to write compositions like she wants them, and we aren't going to be able to get to know the kids in that class any better either. That's why I say it's been a waste of time."

"I see you're really feeling pretty depressed," Mr. Stanford said softly.

"But wait a minute, Shari," Mark said. "We already know each other. Don't you think that we'll all still be friends next fall?"

"I hope so," said Bruce, "but I'm kinda like Shari. I'm afraid it's not going to last through the summer and that I'm not going to be able to do it again either. I just don't think it's the sort of thing you can make happen more than once."

It is the last week of school, and the students, in addition to showing the usual signs of restlessness, are voicing concerns that they never had to face before. A pleasant and valuable experience is coming to an end, and the students are feeling sad and bewildered and even angry. They are struggling with the anxiety of separating themselves from one another and having to face the fact that a profound experience is almost over. They are going through the last stage of life as a group—termination.

CHARACTERISTICS OF THE TERMINATION STAGE

About the only thing that can be said for certain about a classroom group is that it has a beginning and an end. Even if no attention whatsoever is given to the process of group development, a class still starts and ends, sometimes well, sometimes poorly. The Termination Stage is therefore inevitable, no matter what interventions a teacher may or may not make to help the group mature. It occurs regardless of what previous stages the group may have gone through. A class that has developed no further than the Orientation Stage will still go through a termination period, just as surely as will one that achieved productivity. However, there will be qualitative differences in their Termination Stages. A class that has never developed into a group will probably go through a relatively uneventful Termination Stage. Since the students have probably not established deep emotional ties with one another, leaving the class involves no great loss. In fact, members of this underdeveloped class will probably be happy that the year or semester has come to a close. They're often relieved to be released from a none-too-satisfying experience.

On the other hand, the class that has progressed steadily through all stages of group development—the class that has become a *group* in the technical sense—is likely to go through a rather stormy Termination Stage, and the teacher should be prepared to intervene properly. This is, actually, a small price to have to pay for developing a class into a group: students have become tied to one another emotionally and it is harder for them to separate at the end.

In a well developed group, the following symptoms of termination anxiety are likely to appear:

1. Increased Conflict.

Students may start bickering with one another for no

apparent reason, or at least no significant reason. It is almost as though they were trying to prove to themselves that "I don't really like these people—else I wouldn't be fighting with them. And since I don't like them, it won't be painful for me to leave them."

2. Breakdown of Group Skills.

Working together on a task, the group may suddenly exhibit what appears to be a complete lack of skills, and they may violate all the norms that were established in Stage Two. It is almost as though they were saying to themselves and the teacher, "You see— we really didn't change much this year. We're still like every other class. And since this is like every other class, it won't be so hard to leave."

3. Lethargy.

Some students begin to show less and less interest in their work, as if to say, "What does it matter any more? If we're going to have to break up, what's the use of continuing to work?" Their lethargy may also be a sympton of depression, indicating feelings of sadness about the imminent breakup of the group. For example, Janet, normally a highly motivated student, wrote in her journal the last week of school:

> *I can't get myself to do anything. I'm so tired of all the homework that I don't care anymore. I'm going to miss the kids an awful lot, so I don't want it to end, but the work has got to go!*

4. Frantic Attempts to Work Well.

Conversely, some groups may actually increase their productivity, taking on more and more projects and rushing to do everything they can before the term ends. They may display impeccable group skills, working far more effectively than ever before. Implicit in this behavior may be the message, "If we're a model class, maybe the teacher will like us so much we won't have to leave. Maybe our group can continue forever." Some classes work frantically in order to complete some major project that they can leave behind as a sort of "monument" or tangible evidence of what they accomplished together.

5.   Anger at the Teacher.

The most frustrating symptom is anger at the teacher. This may have several roots: On the one hand, students may be saying, "We're mad that you're making us leave. You are the cause of the end of a good experience. You are causing us pain." On the other hand, by saying, "The experience wasn't a good one. You made us do things we didn't want to do. We didn't learn anything, either," students try to convince themselves that the experience was unpleasant, to avoid the pain of leaving it.

Perhaps nothing is more frustrating to the teacher than this last attitude. For the teacher who has worked very hard to provide a rewarding experience for students, who has shared personal feelings openly and honestly with the group, who has patiently accepted students' negative feelings and shared their problems and their joys—it's almost too much to have a class refuse to acknowledge that the experience was worthwhile. The teacher expects kudos from the students, and instead gets insults. But the teacher will have to try to remember that most of the unhealthy symptoms of termination are attempts by students to deny (unconsciously) that it is painful to have the group come to an end. Confronting sadness directly is a difficult thing for most people, and to avoid it people substitute other reactions that are less painful.

A healthy approach to the sadness of termination encourages students to deal in a straightforward manner with their feelings, rather than denying or distorting them. With teacher guidance, students may be able to acknowledge that they've had a good experience which they feel sad about leaving, accept the inevitability that the group will end, and prepare to move on to other experiences.

HELPFUL TEACHER BEHAVIOR IN THE TERMINATION STAGE

A "good" termination helps students become aware of and express their genuine feelings, tie up loose ends, and resolve to reinvest their emotional energy in future experiences. The following teacher behavior will help students achieve a healthy end to their class life together.

Acknowledge that the group is really ending.

It is no help to reassure the group members that they'll be seeing one another informally in the future, or to plan a reunion party some time after the end of school. Acts such as these encourage students to deny or gloss over the fact that the group as they have known it will not exist again. It's far more helpful to acknowledge that the group is coming to an end, and that you and they feel bad about it. You can model healthy behavior by talking honestly about the forthcoming end of the group and refraining from false reassurances.

Encourage students to express their real feelings related to termination.

If students are given opportunities to express their genuine feelings about having to leave the group, they will be less likely to resort to some of the cover-up methods of coping, such as creating conflict or turning on the teacher in anger. You can model the kind of behavior you want by sending "I" messages about your own feelings about leaving the group: "I'm really going to hate to see you kids go. I've gotten to feel close to you and to like you very much, and it's going to be hard to lose you." You can also use techniques of active listening to reflect and clarify the feelings underlying what they express. Students may have a wide range of feelings about leaving the group which may not be limited to sadness. Some may feel anger; others may be relieved that they will be able to escape from the emotional involvement that being a good group member requires. Most people have a mixture of feelings, and the teacher should be willing to accept all of these feelings.

Help students to review the experience.

Students need an opportunity to put into perspective the many diverse events that have taken place in their group. Thinking back over these events will help students analyze more carefully their real feelings about the group experience, and assess its impact on them personally.

Help the group work out a way to immortalize the experience.

Students want to know that the group has lived its life for a purpose, and they will seek some way to assure its immortality. This is a healthy impulse if the focus is on preserving a memory and not on denying that the group is ending. You can help students understand that the group experience has changed each person's life in significant ways and that these changes will last even if the group breaks up. Students may review the things they have learned in the group that they will be able to apply in future situations.

Some groups may wish to leave behind a more tangible "monument," such as the product of a particularly significant group project, or even something as concrete as a tree planted in the school yard or a mural painted on the wall in one of the corridors. Help them find the particular way their group would like to fill this need.

Explore ways students can begin to reinvest their emotional energy.

As the group experience comes to an end, students are left with a great deal of emotional "capital" which needs to be reinvested. Help each student decide what is the best way to do this. Some may want to start to work immediately, helping to improve the group process in a social or religious organization they belong to. Others can think ahead to future classes, and may want to explore ways they can utilize the skills they learned in this group to improve future group experiences.

Tie up any loose ends.

Students need the opportunity to clear up any "unfinished business" they may have within the group. Some may feel the need to express gratitude to the group for its acceptance of them; others may wish to apologize to individuals whom they may have offended in the past; still others may wish to explain certain aspects of their behavior that they did not feel free to discuss previously. It's best to end the group with as little as possible left hanging.

STRUCTURED EXPERIENCES FOR THE TERMINATION STAGE

These activities provide a structured means of achieving the objectives that make for a healthy termination.

1.   Remember When.

Conduct a discussion with the class tracing the group's

development from the first day until the present. Use a time line drawn on the board to depict the group's life, marking the various periods (stages of development) and important events as the group remembers them. Encourage students to share their perceptions of what happened to their class on its way to maturity, recalling events that were particularly meaningful to them. Allow students to ask you any questions they may have about your perceptions of the changes that took place in the group or about things you liked and disliked about the experience.

2. Best Thing That Happened.

Using the *Round Robin* format described in the Orientation Stage (see page 68), have each student tell the class what he or she thinks was the best thing that happened during the year.

3. Santa Claus.

Go around the circle, giving each student an opportunity to give an imaginary gift to another member of the group. Remind students to think of things that they discovered about one another during the year, and to choose a gift that is especially appropriate for that person. For example, Charlie might give Jeff a three-week trip to Kenya, since Jeff has talked incessantly about wishing he could photograph wildlife at close range. Some students will wish to explain their reasons for selecting a particular gift, but do not require that they do so.

4. Changing Impressions.

Have students discuss how their first impressions of one another have changed over the course of the year. If the class is especially responsive, you may merely need to seat them in a circle and ask, "Do you remember how you viewed the people in this group when you entered the class at the beginning of the year (semester, term)? How do you view them now? Can you tell us in what ways your impressions have changed?" With some groups more structure may be needed. You might go around the circle, giving each student a chance to tell one way in which his or her view of another member or of the group as a whole changed. Further structure could be provided by having each student complete the statement, "I used to think . . . but now I think . . ."

5. Time Capsule.

Have the group put together a sort of "Time Capsule," a collection of artifacts that describe their unique characteristics as a group. Tell them you want a person who looks through this collection ten years from now to be able to discern what this group was like and what made the group special. Artifacts might include their photographs, samples of their work (results of any projects, reports of any special tasks they've completed), poems about the group, a collage made from pictures and words cut from magazines, a small stuffed toy animal representing the group mascot, any item symbolizing special interests or activities of the group (e.g., a cookie jar for a group whose members took turns bringing baked treats for the class each Friday).

6. Applying Skills.

Conduct a discussion of how students can apply the interpersonal skills they have learned in this class to future classes. Have them suggest ways in which even one person can affect the process of group development—for example: by suggesting the group members introduce themselves, or by modeling effective listening skills, or by confronting problems openly. Set up role-playing situations in which the students experiment with ways they can apply their skills in the future. For example, "Imagine that you've reported to your American history class on the first day of the new semester. The teacher has finished checking the class list and has issued textbooks. Ten minutes remain before the period ends. The teacher announces, 'Well, that's all we need to do today. Why don't you spend the remaining time looking through your new book?' What needs to happen at this point in that class? What could you, an individual student, do to try to bring that about?"

7. Roles We Played.

Suggest the group discuss what kinds of roles various members have played in the group and what they have given to and received from one another while working together. Seat the class in a circle and lead an open-ended discussion, with students volunteering their ideas. Help students explore what part each member played in the group—e.g., who provided leadership, who shared information, who kept their spirits up with humor, as well as any other special ways in which individuals contributed to the success of the group. Students might say, for example, "Charlie, you always volunteered to write down things when we were working on a project," or "Doris, it was sure neat the way you always managed to talk your father into selling us stuff wholesale," or "Cathy, it sure made me feel good the way you always spoke to me whenever I came into class, even if I was grouchy or preoccupied," or "Terry always insisted that we think through decisions carefully so that we didn't jump to conclusions—remember?"

8. Positive Messages.

Give each student small slips of paper equal to the number of people in the class. On each slip, have students write a brief message to every other person in the group designed to make that person feel good. Suggest that they point out positive things they have noticed about one another during the year. Urge students to be as specific as possible and to try to mention particular events. Leave it optional whether students sign the messages or not. When they've finished, have them fold the slips of paper and write the name of the target person on the outside. Several students can then be designated to deliver the messages to the target persons.

9. Imagining the End.

Ask students to close their eyes and imagine they are leaving the class for the last time. Urge them to become aware of the feelings they are having as they imagine the scene. Then ask them to think of anything they regret not having said or done before they left the class. After a few minutes, tell students to open their eyes. Have them share with the class the kinds of things they were aware of thinking and feeling.

The conclusion of the Termination Stage marks the end of the cycle of group development. Having taken a class through the entire process of growth toward maturity, you are likely to feel no small measure of pride in the accomplishment. But at the same time, there are likely to be regrets that everything did not go exactly as you had hoped. Although it's a temptation to dwell on how you wish you had dealt with the last group differently, this is not the time to look backward. For, as Elisabeth Kubler-Ross writes in the Introduction to *We Are But a Moment's Sunlight*, "Every ending is a bright new beginning." The class that will arrive at the start of the next term will present you with a new opportunity to foster the kinds of group interaction that lead to effective subject-matter learning as well as contributing to the personal growth of both your students and yourself. From each successive experience with group development, you will gain new insights and master new skills.

Hopefully, through this book you have gained a greater understanding of the process of group development and increased competence in group leadership. What effect did the approach have on your class? What activities and procedures worked well? Which were not successful? Do you disagree with the author on any issue? Do you have any questions about group development not answered by the book? The author is eager to hear about your experiences with the suggestions contained in this book.

APPENDIX I: JANET'S EPILOGUE

Note: Six years have passed since Janet made the entries in her personal journal from which I quoted frequently throughout the book. Being curious about what Janet's *current* perceptions of that experience might be, I tracked her down, finally locating her at the University of Arizona where she is enrolled in a pre-med curriculum. She agreed to prepare a brief report about her recollections of her experience in my class and its effects on her. Her report, which I have reproduced here, is not always consistent with my own memories of what happened in Janet's class, or even with what Janet wrote at the time it took place. Despite the inconsistencies, or even perhaps because of them, Janet's report which follows is a valuable source of additional, retrospective information about her experience with group development.

It is very difficult to pinpoint the facets of one's life that have made him the person that he is today. Then, again, it is even more difficult to describe these very personal experiences to someone else, hoping that he can identify with your interpretations. But I am going to attempt the difficult task of depicting one of my very personal experiences, believing that you will be able to appreciate the great impact that it had on me.

Up until six years ago, English class seemed rather uninteresting to me. In fact, the total educational picture of school bored me. It was as if its quite structured curriculum was hindering my chances of working to my capacity. From the time that I ·entered kindergarten, I remember everyone (anyway, it seemed like everyone) lecturing me about the fascinating and enjoyable experiences of school. But I was very frustrated, and somehow unable to discover the "fascinating" adventure. So I sort of let school pass by me, getting practically straight A's with little or no studying. Besides disliking school, I lived the usual traumatic life of an adolescent—braces, the popularity syndrome, confusion about my future and sex, and I am sure that I do not need to continue my list. Due to my uneventful, unrewarding life, I was very disappointed in myself. It was not enough that my parents reminded me of how pretty and smart I was and how proud they were of me. It was important that I feel the same way about myself, and I didn't. I knew that eventually something would happen to make me happy, with a specific goal to reach for, but I could not imagine waiting much longer. It took me only a short time to realize that being a member of Gene Stanford's English class was the beginning of the change.

Cautiously, I entered the class (like I entered all of my classes on the first day), giving everyone the once-over, trying to remember what I had heard about each one, including Mr. Stanford. At this time, a high standing in the popularity rating (the rating made by the Chosen Few) was the criteria for judging others in high school. Disappointed upon noticing that there was nobody "popular" in my class, I just slouched in my chair, feeling another defeat. At the same time, I felt frightened when I heard the explanation of the course. For example, Mr. Stanford asked us to call him "Gene." None of my previous teachers allowed the students to be on a first name basis with them. I struggled to call him Gene throughout the semester, but like many of the members of the class, I failed since I thought that it was disrespectful. As the class progressed, though, my fears subsided, and I began to gain confidence in myself due to the attitudes that Mr. Stanford stressed. He helped the members of the class realize how important everyone's ideas were and not just those who liked to overwhelm the class. This encouraged me to add my opinions. We had countless discussions, and the number of successful ones increased as the semester continued. Honesty and the united opinions of everyone to reach a goal, specified by Mr. Stanford, constituted a successful discussion. Whenever I reminisce about the class, I recall the discussions concerning the "fallout shelter" and the "secret." In the former talk, the class had to imagine the aftermath of a nuclear war. There was one fallout shelter and the entire class was forced to resolve which few of us were worthy enough to stay alive in the fallout shelter. Of course, the decision was painful. In fact, I do not remember ever finalizing it since we perceived that none of us possessed such undesirable qualities to exclude them from our shelter; I knew that we all cared for each other. The "secret" was tougher for me. Each of us wrote down a secret that no one in the class knew about, and then we passed the notes around randomly. Our responsibility included telling someone else's secret, not knowing whose it was, in the manner that we felt that the person meant it. I cringed at the thought of a member verbalizing mine, but I felt assured that no one would laugh or feel sorry for me since the experience was mutual for all of us.

Soon the group consisted of more than class pals. We began getting together outside of class studies. Even when the class ended, we continuously planned activities together. One of these activities included a farewell picnic for Gene. The very sad goodbye would have been sadder if we were aware that we would hear so little from him again. As the year following our class with Gene passed, the resentfulness towards him increased. We missed his encouragement and unfortunately, felt that he did not care about us any more. We were confused, because we surely knew that he must have cared a lot about the group to influence us on the importance of relationships with others. Unhappily, we admitted that he had his own life to lead and that he allowed us to grow the rest of the way on our own. And I did—I had earned so much confidence that I ran for secretary of my junior class and won, auditioned for the school choir, increased my scope of friends and fell in love, all in one year. Maybe then my ideas were quite idealistic, but I was finally happy. I realized that before I had been missing the close friendships of people in my life. I discovered that popularity was a disgusting way to judge others, and that talking to others and hearing what important ideas they had was a lot more fun than judging people by the gossip that I had heard.

Now I am 21, striving for a medical career. I chose the medical profession in order to remain in close contact with others and to help them to function as happily and healthily as they can. As you can tell, Gene helped me to enjoy myself but above all to enjoy others. All I can say now is thank you, Gene, for aiding me in the realization that people need people and that everyone has something to offer someone else.

APPENDIX II:
RATIONALE FOR
THE MODEL OF
GROUP DEVELOPMENT
PRESENTED IN
THIS BOOK

The concept of group development emerged originally from observations of the changes that occurred naturally in groups over time. Researchers noticed that even when the leader made no attempt to intervene in the developmental process, most groups moved through fairly predictable stages—the more successful groups moving further, the less successful ones becoming arrested in early stages. Systematic observation of groups was undertaken and various researchers formulated their own descriptions of the series of steps a group goes through as it develops.

These descriptions appear on the surface to vary widely; some have three stages, others have as many as seven or eight. Yet beneath the diversity, there is a surprising amount of agreement. In surveying approximately 50 articles dealing with group development in a wide variety of settings, Tuckman[1] found that most researchers agreed that the aggregate first goes through a period of uncertainty in which members try to determine their place in the group and what the "rules" of the situation are going to be. Then, in a phase Tuckman calls "storming," conflicts begin to arise; members resist the influence of the group and rebel against accomplishing the task of the group. If it can overcome the problems of conflict, the group moves into a period of establishing cohesiveness and commitment, discovering new ways to work together and setting norms for behavior. Finally, the group develops proficiency in achieving its goals and becomes more flexible in its patterns of working together.

Two questions arise when we attempt to apply Tuckman's stages to classroom groups. First, in virtually all the research on group development on which Tuckman based his summary, the leader of the group made no attempt to intervene in the group development process. That is, the leader just let things happen in order to see how the group would develop over time. This raises an important question: "Would the developmental process have been different, or at least would it have moved along faster, if the leader had made certain interventions to improve group development?"

Secondly, most of the research on which Tuckman's summary is based was conducted on groups with fairly nondirective leaders. In these groups the leader generally withdrew from the traditional leadership role and placed the major responsibility for the group on the members themselves. Many of the leaders deliberately avoided providing direction to see how the group would respond. Thus, we know very little about what changes in group development would result if the leader—for example, a teacher—chooses to play a more directive role. For example, much of the conflict in Tuckman's

---

[1]Tuckman, B.W. "Developmental Sequence in Small Groups." *Psychological Bulletin*, 63 (1965) 384-399.

"storming" stage is a result of group members becoming angry with the leader for not furnishing direction. Would this stage have occurred when it did, or even have occurred at all, had the leader been more directive?

Because of these problems most descriptions of group development are not applicable in the classroom. Left unanswered are questions such as: Can certain types of activities and teacher behavior increase the likelihood that an aggregate will move through all the stages of group development and become productive? Do these teacher interventions simply speed up the process of group development or do they actually change the type and sequence of the stages the group must go through?

As far as I am aware, the only research that speaks directly to these questions is that of Stiltner.[2] She monitored the group development of a number of junior high school classes in a variety of subjects in order to compare the differences in group development between experimental groups, in which the teacher made group development interventions, and control groups which were taught by the same teachers in the conventional way. In contrast to the group leaders in most of the studies reported by Tuckman, the teachers in Stiltner's study played a traditional leadership role and did not assume a nondirective role for the sake of forcing the participants to assume responsibility for the group.

The mass of data which Stiltner collected tends to support the following conclusions: With traditional teacher leadership, the typical junior high class does not become a productive group during the course of a semester unless group development interventions are made. The interventions have the effect of postponing the "storming" stage. Stiltner's experimental groups (those in which teachers made group develop-

[2]Stiltner, Barbara. *The Effects of Interaction Activities and Teacher Role on Group Development in Junior High School Classrooms.* Unpublished doctoral dissertation, University of Colorado, 1973.

ment interventions) never entered a storming stage during the semester she collected data on them. Control classes, by contrast, entered a storming stage early in the semester and then became less negative as the weeks went on.

Stiltner's findings suggest a somewhat revised description of what happens to group development when a class is taught by a traditionally directive teacher who intervenes in a systematic way to improve the group's functioning. The revised model that results, based on both Tuckman's and Stiltner's findings, is the one presented in this book (see chart on page 31).

The Orientation Stage is roughly equivalent to Tuckman's "forming" stage. It is followed by a period during which the group, with the teacher's help, works out patterns and procedures for working together. This Norm Establishment Stage roughly corresponds to Tuckman's "norming" stage. If the Norm Establishment Stage is successfully completed, the classroom group is likely to enter a period of conflict that is roughly equivalent to Tuckman's "storming" stage. The difference is that most of the conflict reported by Tuckman resulted from group members being forced to cope with a nondirective leader. In the model presented in this book, the conflict stage results from norms, such as open communication, established in the Norm Establishment Stage. The Productivity Stage is similar to Tuckman's "performing" stage. The final difference in the model presented here is the inclusion of a Termination Stage, which is absent from Tuckman's model. Since a group's behavior almost always changes in certain predictable ways as it enters the final days or weeks of its life, I have felt it important to consider this period a distinct stage, even though most other writers do not.

ADDITIONAL RESOURCES

Association of American Geographers and the American Sociological Association, *Experiences in Inquiry*. Boston, Allyn and Bacon, Inc., 1974. Contains 12 inquiry-oriented activities, including "Dilemma of the Tribes" for studying cooperation.

Boocock, Sarene E. and E. O. Schild, *Simulation Games in Learning*. Beverly Hills, Sage Publications, Inc., 1968. A basic introduction to using simulations in the classroom.

Chesler, Mark and Robert Fox, *Role-Playing Methods in the Classroom*. Chicago, Science Research Associates, 1966. Good examination of the ways to structure role-playing activities for the study of subject matter.

Citizenship Education Project, *Laboratory Practices in Citizenship: Learning Experiences in the Community*. New York, Citizenship Education Project (Teachers College, Columbia University, New York, NY 10027), 1958. An undiscovered gem of a book, almost twenty years old but amazingly up-to-date. Contains hundreds of ideas for how students can learn about a wide range of topics using the community as a laboratory.

Cromwell, Chester R., William Ohs, Albert E. Roark and Gene Stanford, *Becoming: A Course in Human Relations*. Philadelphia, J. B. Lippincott Company, 1975. A multi-media package of materials for structuring classroom experiences to help students better understand themselves and improve their relationships with others. Divided into three self-contained modules: Relating, Interaction and Individuality. Each module includes a Leader's Guide, Personal Log for students, and kit containing cassettes, photocards and other materials.

Gordon, Thomas, *T.E.T.: Teacher Effectiveness Training*. New York, Peter H. Wyden, 1974. Superb set of specific suggestions for improving communication between teacher and student.

Harmin, Merrill, Howard Kirschenbaum and Sidney B. Simon. *Clarifying Values Through Subject Matter*. Minneapolis, Winston Press, 1973. Description of how values clarification strategies can be adapted to all subject-matter areas.

Hawley, Robert C., *Value Exploration Through Role-Playing*. New York, Hart Publishing Company, 1975. Interesting suggestions for helping students examine their own beliefs and opinions through dramatic activities.

Hawley, Robert C., Sidney B. Simon and D. D. Britton, *Composition for Personal Growth: Values Clarification Through Writing*. New York, Hart Publishing Company, 1973. Contains many fine ideas for linking writing activities to the personal concerns of students.

Hunter, Elizabeth, *Encounter in the Classroom*. New York, Holt, Rinehart and Winston, 1972. Contains a number of useful strategies to improve the relationships among students.

Jones, John E. and J. William Pfeiffer, *The Annual Handbook for Group Facilitators*. La Jolla, University Associates Press, 1972, 1973, 1974, 1975, 1976. Collections of a variety of resources for the group leader, including structured experiences.

Nesbitt, William A., Norman Abramowitz and Charles Bloomstein, *Teaching Youth About Conflict and War*. Washington, D.C., National Council for the Social Studies, 1973. Includes, among other activities, "The Oil Islands Dispute: A Classroom Game of Conflict and Cooperation."

Oliver, Donald W. and Fred M. Newmann, *Taking a Stand: A Guide to Clear Discussion of Public Issues*. Columbus, Xerox Education Publications (Education Center, Columbus, OH 45216), 1967. Suggestions for helping students engage in more profitable discussions in social studies classes.

Paine, Doris M. and Diana Martinez, *The Leader's Guide for Social Action*. New York, Bantam Books (666 Fifth Avenue, New York, NY 10019), 1973. Practical guide to organizing a student group to attack social problems.

Pearson, Craig, *Resolving Classroom Conflict*. Pala Alto, Learning Handbooks, 1974. Suggestions for dealing with disruptive behavior, especially in the elementary school.

Pfeiffer, J. William and John E. Jones, *A Handbook of Structured Experiences for Human Relations Training*. La Jolla, University Associates Press, 1969, 1970, 1971, 1972, 1973, 1974, 1975, 1976. A series of collections of activities adaptable to the classroom.

Pomainville, Martha, Cynthia Blankenship and Barbara Stanford, *Possibilities for Reading/Relating.* New York, Learning Ventures (666 Fifth Avenue, New York, NY 10017), 1977. An innovative, group-centered independent reading program, flexible enough for use in both traditional and open-classroom settings. Each of 15 three-week units, designed for groups of five to fifteen students, is based on a theme ranging from values, communication, and mental illness to popular music, interaction, and sexual identity.

Reichert, Richard, *Self-Awareness Through Group Dynamics.* New York, Cebco Standard Publishing, 1970. Group activities that help students learn about themselves and clarify their opinions on issues such as prejudice, freedom, sexual identity, and the generation gap.

Robert, Marc, *Loneliness in the Schools.* Niles, Argus Communications, 1974. Examines the way many schooling practices isolate students from one another and from the teacher and isolate teachers from other teachers, and suggests alternatives to these conditions.

Schmuck, Richard A. and Patricia A. Schmuck, *Group Processes in the Classroom.* Dubuque, Wm. C. Brown Company, 1971. A clear, easily understood explanation of the basic principles of group dynamics, applied to the classroom. Considers issues such as leadership, attraction, norms, communication, cohesiveness and developmental stages.

Schmuck, Richard A. and Patricia A. Schmuck, *A Humanistic Psychology of Education: Making the School Everybody's House.* Palo Alto, National Press Books, 1974. A comprehensive, largely theoretical guide to humanizing the school through changes at all levels from classroom to administration.

Shaftel, Fannie R. and George Shaftel, *Role Playing for Social Values.* Englewood Cliffs, Prentice Hall, Inc., 1967. Provides some explanation of how to use role-playing, followed by a useful collection of open-ended stories through which students can explore their values on social issues.

Simon, Sidney B., Leland W. Howe and Howard Kirschenbaum, *Values Clarification.* New York, Hart Publishing Company, 1972. A collection of 79 activities for helping students think and talk about their own beliefs, opinions and values.

Stanford, Gene and Albert E. Roark, *Human Interaction in Education.* Boston, Allyn and Bacon, Inc., 1974. Offers both theory and practical techniques for humanizing education, including new approaches to group discussion, role-playing, simulation games, personal involvement with the subject matter and activities beyond the classroom.

Stanford, Gene and Barbara Dodds Stanford, *Learning Discussion Skills Through Games.* Englewood Cliffs, Citation Press, 1969. A handbook of activities to develop a group's ability to handle discussions more profitably and enjoyably.

Zeleny, Leslie D., *How to Use Sociodrama.* Washington, D.C., National Council for the Social Studies (1201 Sixteenth Street, N.W., Washington, D.C. 20036), 1964. Specific guidelines for the utilizing of role-playing and other dramatic approaches in the social studies class.